THE ECADEMY GU
POWER NETWORKING

NETWORKING FOR LIFE

BY

THOMAS POWER

MAY 2003

Networking for Life

© Thomas Power

First published May 2003 by

ecademy Press
1 Rothwell Grange Court,
Rothwell Road, Kettering
Northamptonshire NN16 8FB

Internet: www.ecademypress.com

Wonderful book! Clearly written from the heart of a master with excellent information on the philosophy, habits, attitude and skills for a fulfilling and contributing networking lifestyle. This book exemplifies and supports the magnitude of networking as a positive means for making a difference in our world.

Donna Fisher, author of *Power Networking, People Power, Power NetWeaving* **and** *Professional Networking for Dummies.*

In a few years, everyone will recognise personal networking as a basic skill, a social literacy without which we will struggle to get by in life, even less be able to get on in business. Thomas Power has networked himself to death so that you don't have to, and very kindly put what he has learnt down on paper. It is hard to think of anyone in any career or stage of their life who would not benefit from knowing this book.

Charles Cohen, author of *Corporate Vices,* **entrepreneur and founder of Beenz.com.**

Lots of people claim to enjoy networking, but alongside Thomas they're all amateurs: he's a people collector! Thomas lives networking and, through his development of Ecademy, he is helping to redefine networking. For several years now I've been regularly challenged by Thomas, and through this process I've developed a stronger awareness of how and why I network. This book gives you access to that knowledge. It will also give you the framework to think afresh about how you live your life through networking.

Bill James, director of BT.com and founding director of ThomasCook.com.

Networking For Life gives deep insight into Thomas's passion for networking and its great power to change our lives. Networking has already brought me many new opportunities, and Thomas's book will help many others to embrace networking and open up new opportunities for them. The book also reflects what I have come to know and respect about Thomas: that he is a firm and committed believer in the power of people networks, and a leader in the appreciation and development of this power.

Deon Erwee, Entrepreneur and Project Management Consultant, Culture Consulting Limited.

Thomas Power is the UK's leading networker. He networks for life so you don't have to. I recommend everyone studies both his methods and results.

David Taylor, author of *The Naked Leader*.

In *Networking for Life*, Thomas Power demonstrates in vivid Technicolor how lives can be changed by just getting out there and meeting people. Thomas is a fun guy who describes in a fun way how to step over the threshold, become a networker and enjoy the fruits of connecting with others. Anyone who reads *Networking for Life* will learn how to build their personal networking balance sheet, with "give" on one side and "take" on the other.

Tony Rice, BT.

Emotional intelligence is an amazing science but seeing it in action is altogether a different thing. Networking tends to bring this intelligence to life.

Thomas Power has reached many people through the use of technology yet he himself does not come across as an early adopter of technology – this may be proven by his preference for a sketchbook as used by Van Gogh as opposed to a tablet PC – he does however use video conferencing and other forms of communication. He is a communication addict.

This passion has helped Thomas become witness to the change taking place in modern society and in particular in how society does business. His exposure to board level decision making by public companies, running businesses in the SME sector, association with various online communities and contacts from all over the world in a diverse range of industries have kept him finely tuned as to what is happening - not what will happen perhaps but what IS happening now.

Thomas would never have been able to do this without networking or his superb business networking tool: www.ecademy.com. His book is a testament to this achievement.

Ed Daniel, Entrepreneur.

In spite of being an e-commerce expert and running one the world's largest online business networks, Thomas is a tireless advocate for exceedingly human values – generosity, respect, trust, and personal development. As a result, while this book is extremely timely considering the current economy and the explosion of inexpensive global communications, it is also timeless in its wisdom. Anyone exploring business networking should read this to help them keep their priorities straight.

Scott Allen, OnlineBusinessNetworking.com and About.com Entrepreneurs Guide.

Contents

Introduction

Why you should read this book

The business world is making a gentle sucking sound. Can you hear it? It's been going on for a couple of years now. The sound is partly made up of the hiss of escaping hype as the dotcom bubble continues to deflate. Another element of the sound is the clicking of dropped jaws as once-proud companies admit to failures of governance, and retreat from the stage. And the last part is a kind of whimpering: a mass cry of hunger as people and companies yearn for a new beginning, a new direction, a new set of hopes.

Networking is the Next Big Thing that will satisfy the hunger. Networking is also a Very Old Thing that's always been with us – driving markets, satisfying our personal and social needs, and making us human.

This book is about networking as a business tool, but more importantly as a life skill. I believe that networking is *the* basic skill of our age. I believe it's the single-most important skill that you need to practise.

I am a committed networker. It's stamped on my forehead. In 2002, I had 1,300 meetings with people. I live and breathe networking. And I think about it, study it, and search for ways to improve the way I do it.

Through the networking organisation I co-founded, Ecademy, I encounter thousands of people and share in their goals, their frustrations and their joys. I soak these encounters up. In this book, I distil what I've learned in many combined lifetimes of networking.

Like most authors, I wrote this book because I wanted to read it, and it didn't yet exist. I'm also privileged to be connected to a great number of people who continually ask me for my tips on networking, and for my philosophy of networking. I've tried to do both things in this book, combining practical approaches to the habits of networking with deeper explorations of why networking is important, and how it is changing our world.

By reading this book, you'll fuel yourself with the equivalent of many hundreds of person-years of networking experience. You'll learn why you need to network, and how you can go about networking. You'll learn that networking doesn't involve pretending to be anything you're not, going against any of your values or exploiting anyone. On the contrary, you'll learn that networking is about being yourself, and enjoying yourself.

But above all you'll be preparing yourself for the rest of your career in a changed, accelerated and unpredictable business world.

Networking will provide you with ways of formulating and achieving your goals. It will expand your horizons, and make your world more fascinating. And it will put food on your table, and light in your eyes.

You'll also find that as you embrace networking, and integrate networking in your daily life, that the painful sounds of a wounded business age begin to fade away.

Networking makes a great sound that drowns it out. It's the sound of us all working together in harmony, with each other and for each other. Now that's something worth listening to – and joining in.

How to use this book

Mark this book. Fold the pages, underline things, write in the margins. I want you to engage with this book while you read it. When we meet (as we inevitably will), I don't want to see this book on your shelf. I hope you'll have absorbed its message, and taken the parts you need. And if you can't bear to tear it up, at least pass it on to someone else for them to read. (You could even leave it on a bus or in a café for a stranger to find: see www.bookcrossing.com.)

I also want you to email me. Tell me what you find helpful in the book. Tell me where I'm wrong. Tell me what you want to see in the next edition. Tell me about how networking is affecting your life and business. Share your experiences of the joys of networking, the maths of networking, and the rewards of networking. Network with me! You can email me at thomas.power@ecademy.com, or phone me on my mobile at +44 (0)7976 438285.

Or become a Power Networker at Ecademy and book a personal session at my regular Monday surgery in central London.

I've written the book in British English. American readers will want to read "specialty" for "specialism", and can be reassured that when "Dorking" appears in my *Fifty Words* (see Chapter 2), I'm referring to a town in the south-east of England and not some sexual practice that might be outlawed in one or more of the States.

I also like to roughly split infinitives, and to finish sentences with words they shouldn't be finished with. These decisions won't win prizes for grammar, but they help me to keep a natural tone.

By the way, I use "he" and "she" at random throughout the text. I haven't kept score, so if the girls appear to be doing better than the boys, or vice versa, don't read anything into it.

Thanks

I thank the 20,000 members of Ecademy. You are my teachers.

I thank Paul May for helping to prepare the manuscript. I thank Donna Fisher, Scott Allen, John Colley, Charles Cohen and David Taylor who read draft versions and made many helpful comments that resulted in a stronger and clearer book. I also thank those networkers and colleagues who have most influenced the approach set out in this book: Julie Meyer, Neil Holloway, Pierre Danon, Mike Southon, Tony Rice, Brent Hoberman, Mark Zaleski,

George Jerjian, Bill James, Michael Harrison, Maggy Whitehouse, Carole Stone and Freddie McMahon.

I thank Glenn Watkins, our CEO, and his wife Sophia; John Bromley, our CFO and my personal assistant; Julian Bond, our CTO and code-cutter extraordinaire; and Leon Benjamin, our Head of Consulting and thinker of genius.

And my thanks, as ever, go to Penny – not least for inventing Ecademy, but also for being the wind beneath my wings; and to our children Hannah, Ross and TJ, who remind me daily that our greatest task in life is to pass on what we learn to those we love.

Chapter 1

The Richer Your Networks, the Greater Your World

The power is in the links

> Now I'm the king of the swingers
> Oh, the jungle VIP
> I've reached the top and had to stop
> And that's what botherin' me

> *I Wan'na Be Like You* by Richard M. Sherman and Robert B. Sherman

We spend our lives in a hurry to achieve. To reach ever higher. Our language is full of climbing and clambering. We drive ourselves to "peak performance", we fear "career plateaux" and we dread being "on the skids".

Yet you rarely find a professional who will admit to having reached the top of his climb, and being satisfied with his position. (And yes, we are usually – sadly – talking of "him".)

The king of the monkeys in Disney's *Jungle Book* isn't satisfied with his domain in the jungle – nor his excellent house band. He wants to conquer another peak. He wants to change species.

It seems that when we've reached the top, we can either deny that we've arrived, or try to start again. In either case, we reject the place we are in. It's as if, having achieved a longed-for goal, we no longer value it when we hold it.

Perhaps we need some new ideas about tops.

Top stop

Take five minutes to answer these questions for yourself.

- Have you reached "the top"?
- Is this the "top" you wanted?
- Are you proud of your position?
- Do you use your position to develop others on the same journey?
- Do you use your position to return value to the community?
- What do you see when you look down – the difficult trail you took, a sudden drop to failure, pretenders in pursuit?

Travelling in Style

When people are dissatisfied with success, it's often because they have achieved goals that were never really dear to them.

They've done a great job in becoming something they never wanted to be. They've lived someone else's life.

This happens to everyone. It's inevitable in early life, when you're making sense of the world by imitating people around you. Children try to be like the adults and peers they admire. Sometimes they react strongly against adult models, particularly in the teenage years. In either case, we're creating our characters in response to the people we see around us.

There comes a time when we leave these strategies behind, and become our own person. In bygone times, ceremonies marked the passage to adulthood. Few of these rituals survive. With lengthening education and increasing leisure, it's possible to postpone the transition to adulthood for longer and longer. And if you join a large organisation, you'll probably find yourself slotted into a structure that tells you how to behave.

Then one day, you wake up and wonder why you're living the life you're living. Why you do the job you do. It's hard to pinpoint exactly where you took the decisions that led to this point.

The thing is: you didn't take the decisions.

Imagine that you set out to drive across a big city. You have no particular destination in mind. But everyone's driving across the city, so that's what you do. Each time you encounter traffic at a standstill, you turn off on the first available road. When you reach a junction, you follow the route that looks easiest. Where do you end up?

Imagine instead that you have a firm idea of your destination. You work out the optimum route before you leave home, and you stick to it. You don't yield an inch in road space to anyone else. You're going to win this battle. You reach your goal.

Both these travellers fail.

The first traveller participates in the life of the city, but arrives at a destination by chance. She'll never know if she's in the "right" place. In fact, she hasn't asked what's "right" for her. Any place is good enough when you have no place in mind.

The second traveller looks like a go-getter. But she's all competition. She sticks to a goal that she set before she even entered the city. She never explores the millions of other destinations open to her. And she treats her fellow citizens as competitors.

This isn't travelling. If you don't have a goal, it's meandering. If you stick to a single goal, it's racing.

An old ad for cruise ships used to say: *Getting there is half the fun.* I'd go further than that. I say: *The journey is the whole point.*

Positions and Journeys

The position you hold is not a thing: it's something you do. You can be appointed to a prestigious role, but unless you perform in that role, you'll only be a placeholder.

If your position is something you do, rather than something you are, then it follows that your position must be constantly changing, depending on what you're doing. This is great news, because it means that your position is no longer constrained. There are some physical and human laws that you'd be well advised not to break, but otherwise you make your own life.

It's worth abandoning the concept of "position", and replacing it with ideas about "process". It's not where you are in some hierarchy that counts, but how you use your abilities, and how you interact with the people around you.

If process is a more useful concept than position, then we should be putting our energy into creating good processes. Another way of putting this is to say: Life should be made up of great experiences, not luggage labels.

In this book, we look at how you can change who you are by changing what you do. There's no mystery or trickery involved – no deep breathing, no chanting, no tree-hugging. I've developed this approach amongst cynical Brits, and it works just as well in the English drizzle as it does under a Californian sun.

Is your ladder against the right wall?

- Can you trace the decisions you took that led to your current position? Draw each decision point as a dot, and draw an arrow to show how each decision led to the next.

- What alternate paths were open to you? At each decision point, draw at least one alternate arrow. How would you label the alternate destination? What paths does the alternate destination open up?

Room at the Top

It's a mistake to think that there's only one "top", and that there's only room for a handful at the top. There is, in fact, more than enough room in the world for everyone to have their own top, or a succession of tops.

Ecademy members have traversed many tops in their lifetimes. They have scaled the heights of massively different industries, professions and organisations. They have also mastered incredible ranges of lifeskills, from parenthood to entrepreneurship, from personal resilience to citizenship.

Many Ecademists have discovered that the fundamental truths of networks make a nonsense of traditional "top-oriented" thinking. It's not that hierarchies are bad in themselves. It's just that hierarchies don't adequately explain how we can achieve what we want in business, and in life. They aren't rich enough to express all the possibilities that exist to us. Hierarchical thinking is constrained thinking.

Nodes and Links

When we measure the world only in terms of tops, we ignore its more complex structure. And the simple truth behind any concept of a "top" is that of relationships.

Spatial relationships, power relationships, commercial relationships – every type of interface known to our sociable and inventive species.

In the language of networks, a top is a *node*. A node is simply a place where relationships meet. A road junction is a node between two or more roads. An airport is a node amongst many routes and flights.

Nodes exist in space and time. So, while an airport is a fixed node in space, it truly functions as a node only during the flying day.

In the same way, people can – and do – act as nodes. Some human nodes are so important to our cultures that they have honoured roles in our communities. The pastor, for example, acts as a node amongst believers, inhabiting a clear space and time at which people can come together in common cause. Other examples of honoured human nodes include judges and teachers.

Some nodes are fixed, while others are nomadic. As the rate of change in our society continues to increase, we find more nomadic roles than fixed ones. In business, the nodes that control access to funding or customers change depending on market conditions. These nomadic nodes differ from appointed or elected nodes, like law officers or politicians, but they are no less significant in the networked world. In fact, the variability introduced into networks by nomadic nodes enriches the power of those networks.

They make networks more diverse and less predictable, which in turn increases the collective creativity of the network and the number of opportunities it spawns for its members.

The node role is arguably the fastest growing cultural phenomenon in the modern world. Customer care agents, call centre workers and other customer-facing staff are all essentially human nodes. They bring together customers with the organisations that serve them. It's the job of nodes to make those relationships persist, and to make them work. Without nodes, we are adrift.

The connections between nodes are most easily called *links*. The name has a clear role in transport networks, where we talk of rail links or road links between cities. We also talk naturally of our links with our employers, our friends, our families and our hometowns.

Our links anchor us in the social world. They also provide our most valued means of communication.

The growing significance of networks in all areas of life has led some researchers, thinkers and commentators to identify a "new science of networks". We'll be looking at some of their ideas later in the book.

The Power is in the Links

We have become used to the false idea that people are at the mercy of communications. We believe that audiences passively consume messages beamed at them by a powerful media complex.

We organise our political life around representative parties, and formalised debates between champions. It's as if our communications tasks are handled by wiser beings – packaged and orchestrated for our consumption.

The truth is that communications belong to us all. Conversing is our birthright. And we do not willingly restrict our conversations to one-way exchanges. Communicating creates links. The more we communicate, the wider and stronger our networks are. *And the richer our networks, the greater our world.*

The Internet has had a remarkable effect in opening up communications, especially through email. Yet the media's use of the Internet has tended to emphasise the one-to-many broadcast model. This is so even where a media concern personalises its sites for the user. The communications model is still heavily centred on "content" – as if the only value in a communications channel is its function as a bearer of consumable messages.

In fact, Internet technologies allow individuals to converse and transact without any help from media companies. The phenomenal success of first Napster and then KaZaA in enabling music swapping is being emulated in other peer-to-peer initiatives. And in the telecoms industry, where the mobile revolution is moving into a data-enhanced era, the technology has always been person-to-person.

Cheap, ubiquitous communications technologies are fuelling an era-defining shift towards networking as the de facto, explicit enabler of human society. And the more we communicate, the more powerful we become.

From a business point of view, networking is the new marketing. Automated word-of-mouth (or word-of-mouse!) is a key means of creating attention and gaining customers for new products and services. Marketers who neglect to immerse themselves in the burgeoning conversational world of mobile phone texting, email, instant messaging and weblogs absent themselves from the richest and most active commercial environment that the world has ever seen. In today's world, you've got to talk *with* people, not *at* them.

Your volume

Write down your answers to these questions, and put today's date next to them. Update the figures after you've finished this book, and then again a month later.

- How many people do you have in your personal network?

- How many new contacts do you make in a week?

- How many meetings do you have in a week?

- How much of your time is spent online as opposed to offline?

Reaching for Richness

In the rest of this book, we look at the world in terms of nodes and links. We navigate a world whose architecture is fluid, changeable. It's an exciting place that offers new opportunities and new challenges to us all. It is a world of richness in which no one need ever reach the top and have to stop. Networkers carry on growing, learning, collecting and sharing. Take these simple ideas about nodes and links to heart, and you'll start to see their principles at work wherever you look. And soon you'll recognise yourself as part of a powerful, all-encompassing network that comprises our new economy, and our new culture.

Chapter 2

Being Stranded

The world isn't divided into frogs and frog-princes. It's all princes.

This chapter is about how you can shift from being stuck as a solitary person to being a part of a network. I introduce the concept of professional loneliness, a little-known but powerful, silent killer of careers. I show why networking isn't the flaky, semi-sleazy activity you might think it is, but how it actually is (and isn't) rocket science.

Then I'll stop your head spinning, and show you how value flows through networks. There are five keys for you to collect during this part of the journey. Each key opens a door to good networking practice. The five keys are:

1. Be aware that you are a node.

2. Take responsibility for all your communications.

3. Describe yourself in fifty words.

4. Maintain your link neighbourhood.

5. Be open to random encounters.

We'll also look at how people get to know each other, and how you can make the process of learning about people more efficient and effective. I introduce the powerful "fifty words" tool, and take a cool look at frogs and princes. Along the way, I demolish as many myths about networking as I can find, and demonstrate why networking is the most natural thing in the world.

Stranded at the Top

I have a phrase for the sense of isolation that goes along with being stranded at "the top". It's *professional loneliness.*

Professional loneliness is a state that afflicts many, many people. It's not the same as other kinds of loneliness – social, emotional or sexual – though it shares some characteristics with those feelings. It's more like a self-imposed limitation, caused by a faulty view of "tops".

In a world of niches, we can all find ourselves at the top of our specialism. And it's always lonely at the top. Whether you're a board director of a large company, a country pastor or the best skater at the rink, you occupy a seemingly unique position. You have no one to share your insights, frustrations or doubts with.

But consider this: in a networked world, every "top" is just a node. Your "top" is an entry point to a rich, planet-girdling network of people.

The expertise and experience that defines your "top" is potential fuel for new conversations, new friends and new opportunities. Shift your thinking from "top-ism" to "node-ism" and the world becomes exciting again.

If you think of your current position as a niche, then you're in a prison. Your niche might protect you from the rain, but you can't carry it about with you like an umbrella. You're stuck with your local glory.

And if you think of your position as a peak, then the only way you *can* move is downwards. Creating connections across tops is a way of creating a plateau. Once you acknowledge that the professional world is a landscape of tops, and that you can bridge the gaps between distant peaks, you have the power to erase professional loneliness from your life. You'll replace dizziness with ease, isolation with solace.

Professional loneliness is the Number One inhibitor of success in today's business environment. It blocks the value that otherwise flows freely through networks. And its personal effects can be tragic. Your career can die of professional loneliness.

The good news is that professional loneliness can be conquered. It isn't hard to dispel. But in order to remove it, we need to know where it comes from.

So, how do we acquire professional loneliness?

It happens like this. On your way to your top, you gradually lost the opportunities and the motivation to chat with people around you.

At some point, your career ambitions overshot the water cooler. You lost the sense of village life that brought colour and warmth to your working day. Once lost, that sense of camaraderie is hard to find again. Its true value is only felt when it has gone.

When we reach our chosen top, we rarely relish the view for long. Soon, a sense of isolation sets in. To people on the lower slopes, we seem unapproachable – perhaps even another species. We may have "made it", but we've lost something too. We have gained visibility, status and power – at the cost of belonging, contributing and nurturing.

That's professional loneliness: a state where peer relationships have been jettisoned – like rockets in a moon shot.

Rocket Science

Networking is about replacing races to the moon with reusable craft and meaningful missions. It's about repeatable, sustainable success, rather than breakthrough heroics. Networking is grown-up business.

This view of the world is very different from the one we're used to hearing. We're comfortable with the idea of a well-designed world, with sensible hierarchies and niches, and predictable outcomes. And, perhaps, we'd like to think of "networking" as some form of disguised sales activity – greed dressed in sharp suits and lubricated with champagne.

These stereotypes are holding people back, and condemning them to lives of professional misery. Sometimes people are persuaded of the increasingly networked nature of the world, but dissuaded from joining in by their perceptions of what networking is. They see the best jobs and business opportunities passing them by, their skills becoming less relevant and the demands made on them becoming ever harder – yet they stick with the devil they know. Anything must be better than "being a networker", right?

But wait a minute. I wouldn't want to spend time with the caricatured networker either.

I don't want to be buttonholed and sold to.

I don't want to be pumped for my knowledge and contacts, then dumped in an alley.

I don't want to lose my powers of judgement and embrace every stranger I meet.

I don't want to glow with the eerie light of a cult-believer.

Whatever other tacky, repellent, manipulative, self-seeking or anti-social behaviours you might associate with networking – I don't want any part of them either.

I'm *myself* when I network. I don't disappear into a phone booth, put my underpants on over my trousers and emerge as a different person, and "go networking". I don't recognise any boundary between my networking activities and anything else I do.

I'm on a journey though life, and so is everybody else. I just acknowledge that fact, and enjoy the company.

And I keep – and express – my sense of humour, quirky as it is. I'm not afraid to say, for example, that "networking isn't rocket science" at the same time as I point out that it is. It's not rocket science, because anyone can do it. It is rocket science, because it's about reusable craft and meaningful missions. We could laugh at that together, or argue about it, or dismiss it. It's hardly a sales pitch though, is it? It's not a headlock. It doesn't come with a reply-paid coupon. It's just conversation.

But I know one thing: no one ever got to the moon, powered by a revolving bow tie. Whatever stereotypes you may have about networkers and networking, let them go.

The Flow Of Value

Value flows freely through networks, unless it's blocked by a faulty node or lost in a faulty link. A faulty link is a breakdown in communications between two nodes, so link failures are the responsibilities of nodes as well. To be a part of an effective network, all you have to do is to pay attention to your responsibilities as a node. These responsibilities are serious, but not onerous. Once you're part of a functioning network, you can participate in the value flowing through it.

The first key to behaving as a node is to *be aware that you are a node*. You need to recognise that you haven't "arrived".

You are still journeying, and will be until the day you die – and, some believe, beyond. Whatever top you have reached, you still have peers. And there are still people ahead of you in your journey, people who have scouted the territory ahead and can help you on your way. There are also people in your wake, who are looking to you as a model for their own journeys. And this is true across all the many, many networks that you are a member of.

Key 1: Be aware that you are a node.

How many networks are you in?

- How many people do you know?

- How many networks are you a member of?

- How often do you participate in your networks?

The second key to behaving as a node is to *take responsibility for all your communications*. And I mean *all*. Here's how human communication works: If you communicate something to someone, and they don't receive or understand your message, it's *your* problem, not theirs.

If you mail someone a letter and it doesn't arrive, it's *your* problem. It doesn't matter what happened to the letter, whether it was stolen by aliens or eaten by wild dogs (like some of my homework when I was a kid). You have to find an alternative way to communicate with your recipient. If you've used an unreliable method of communication, then you need to consider going back to a method you trust: face-to-face, person-to-person. Use that telephone!

If you say something to someone else, and they don't understand, it's *your* problem. We don't all see the world the same way: that's what makes life interesting. No one can read your mind. Most of us do our best to read the minds of poor communicators, but we're unlikely to be successful all the time – and it's very, very tiring.

You need to frame your message in the right way for your audience. And that means you've got to learn about your audience before you start communicating. You have to spend some time – perhaps a lot of time – communing with the other person, in an apparently aimless fashion. It's called *getting to know* people, and it's a vital step towards clear communications.

This all takes practice. You need to communicate with lots of people, lots of the time. Every interaction you have is a chance to learn more about people, and about your own style of interaction.

Each conversation helps you become a better listener, and a better empathiser. The best definition of "empathy" I know is the idea of being in the other person's shoes. You can only get that point of view by practising with lots of people – different people, from different backgrounds and with different goals.

Key 2: Take responsibility for all your communications.

Getting To Know You

You may have heard another term going the rounds recently: *interaction anxiety*. Interaction anxiety is the sense of fear that grips people who would rather not deal with other people, thank you very much. Networking strikes fear into the hearts of these folks. They remember that great phrase (and bestselling book title) "do lunch or be lunch" and imagine that networking is a pastime for the aggressive and predatory.[1]

Nothing could be further from the truth.

I'll let you into a secret: *Everyone* experiences interaction anxiety.

Here's another secret: Everyone goes to the bathroom.

The way to work with your interaction anxiety is to shift your thinking away from what other people might think of you, to what you want them to know about you.

This is the essence of the third key to being a good node: knowing who you are, and letting people know it. I've developed a simple technique for this, called *Fifty Words*.

---

[1] Howard Stevenson's book *Do Lunch or Be Lunch: The Power of Predictability in Creating Your Future* (Harvard Business Press, 1997) is actually about creating predictability in business rather than networking.

Fifty words: meet someone in a minute

I believe that a rich portrait of anyone can be made with just fifty words. You can use the fifty words technique to make it easier for people to get to know *you*. Choose fifty words that point to where you've come from, where you're going, and what you value.

It's like laying out a stall in the networking market. It's not like a pitch: your fifty words don't need to sell anything, or make any kind of claim. They're a little like a book's index – a quick route to what's interesting inside!

With fifty words you can meet someone in a minute. And they can meet you in the same minute. Print your fifty words on the back of your business card. That way, your card becomes not just a contact mechanism, but a tiny "user's manual" to you.

Here's the list of fifty words I used in March 2003:

> Solihull, Maths, History, Books, Retail, Sales, Dorking, Tennis, Scout, Walking, Croydon, Finance, Marketing, Aquarius, London, Amstrad, Software, Microsoft, Dell, Wimbledon, Database, Urban Science, Farnham, Married, Children, Football, AKQA, Internet, Debis, Mercedes, BT, Commerce One, eProcurement, Author, Ecademy, Speaker, Non-Executive Director, Dogs, Hotels, Movies, Networking, Harley-Davidson, Cigars, Catholic, Terminator2, Relentless, Views, Meet Joe Black, Lexus, Penny, France, Moments

I review my list regularly, to make sure it still represents me faithfully. But I make very few changes to it. You'll notice I use a mix of business-related words and personal details. They're all part of what makes me me.

I advise you to stick to personal emotive words and phrases: words that lie close to your key personal interests. Lists of products and services are, well, boring. Too many of them, and your fifty words will be crowded out by messages about what you might be selling. (I hope it's obvious from my list that I'm not a roving salesman for Lexus or Harley-Davidson. Although, if either company want to send me some free goodies, they know where to find me.)

The "fifty words" tool is a very powerful instance of the third key to being a good node: *Describe yourself.* Pick your words, and attach them to yourself in every practical way you can.

Words worth

Key 3: Describe yourself in fifty words.

Write down fifty words that will act as link words for people who might want to connect with you.

You might want to use your fifty words in the "keywords" meta-tags of your personal home page on the web.

Ecademy members can enter their fifty words in their personal profile. The site has a function labelled "people like this", so that you can find people with similar interests, based on their fifty word profiles. (There's more on this feature in Chapter 5.)

What Can You Do For Me?

If you take nothing else away from this book, I hope you'll at least want to eradicate the question "What can you do for me?" from your repertoire. Whether you say it out loud to people or just let it echo in your mind, this phrase is the weedkiller of networking. It's pure poison.

Successful networkers make a clear distinction between people and tools. Yes, they use tools to network: scheduling software, voice mails, contact databases, notes about people in their network. But they don't use *people* as tools.

If you see people as puppets, or levers of a money-making machine, you'll find your network disappearing around you. Self-seeking is incompatible with effective networking. It is, literally, *repellent*. It drives people away.

I'm not denying that we all want things out of life. I'm in business to create wealth for my family, to live my chosen lifestyle, and to enjoy building great businesses with great people. But the paths to these outcomes are complex, twisting – and unpredictable.

When you say "What can you do for me?" you are saying: *Relieve me of my journey. I'm too tired to keep going – give me a magic shortcut to my goal.*

When you say "What can you do for me?" you close down your network. This anti-magic spell shrivels links and douses nodes. It advertises that you want your contacts to carry you, and that you're not going to do any free lifting.

The energy in networks arises from a willing suspension of self-interest. When we network, we pool our creativity, energy and appetite for life. We help others without expecting anything in return. We help each other because smart people help each other.

The bottom line is this:

- The more you give, the more you receive.

- The more matchmaking you do, the more matches will be made for you.

- The more knowledge you give away, the more you will learn.

- The more you invest, the more you will earn.

Link neighbourhood maintenance

The fourth key to being a good node is to *maintain your link neighbourhood*. This means you regularly refresh and deepen your own links, and support any other links you know about. Remember, the energy in networks comes from the participants, not from a battery. We all have to keep pedalling, otherwise the lights will flicker and fade. But networks have very efficient gearing: it only takes a *little* input to produce a lot of activity. You keep your links alive by communicating.

Use this checklist to ensure that you maintain your network in good condition.

- When did we last talk?
- When did we last talk about nothing in particular?
- When did we last talk about something I could do for you?

Key 4: Maintain your link neighbourhood.

The Frog-Prince Prediction Machine

Sales people have a saying: *You have to kiss a lot of frogs.* Sales folks swap this wry insight when they've spent a heavy day travelling, pitching and negotiating.

They don't mean it as a complaint. They're just stating a fact.

To meet one new customer, you have to first meet all the people who are going to reject your offer. You have to meet all the people who are really in the market for something other than your product. You have to meet all the people who haven't got the money for your product. You have to meet all the people who haven't thought through what they want. And you have to meet all the people who just like pulling the wings off flies – and who think sales people are bluebottles.

Like a hopeful princess, the sales person kisses frogs in the hopes of finding that elusive prince. It's a good image. It sums up the scale of the task, and hints at the distaste that some people associate with pitching.

It also gets across the idea that customers are truly princes who have merely been cast into a state of invisible dumbness by some magic spell. Your princes are out there somewhere: pucker up!

We're all to some extent in the sales business. Even if we don't have a product or service we'd like to sell, we have an idea that we want people to "buy". We're all looking for frogs to kiss.

More importantly, we're also all frogs – and potential princes – ourselves. That's because we all need things too, whether we know it or not. We're all buyers – *big* buyers. Check your credit card statements if you don't believe me. But our buying activity is largely unconscious. It's pleasurable, natural.

It's harder to think consciously like a buyer than as a seller, but you have to do it. People who network are open to buying: to buying people and ideas. If you don't feel that participation in a network can meet your needs, then you aren't going to be a properly active member. In a healthy network, we all listen to each other. And we are alive to the notion that there might be things we need from other people.

So, in an efficient network, all the nodes are potential princes, and every time a link lights up with a piece of communication – well, that's like a kiss.

Now, this frog-kissing saying is supposed to be a *joke*. Isn't the point of the joke that kissing frogs is a time-consuming, haphazard and frankly unhygienic habit? Shouldn't we be *targeting*? Isn't that what technology is for – zeroing in on likely targets, reducing uncertainty, saving effort?

The fact is, no one has ever built, or *will* ever build, a Frog-Prince Prediction Machine. That's because there is no single characteristic, or set of characteristics, or distinct piece of behaviour, or experimental procedure or anything else that can reveal the prince among a field of frogs.

Even if you can describe your ideal prince to the smallest degree, you won't be able to find him amongst the frogs, unless you go a-wooing. That's because your ideal prince – your ideal customer, your prime demographic – is an abstraction, or even a mirage. He's not a real prince.

Direct marketing and predictive modelling methods have been in use for thirty years now – and have produced practically nothing in the way of results. It's time to let those approaches go.

Remember, your needs are constantly changing too. If you've got a fixed idea of what a prince looks like, you'll likely miss a vast range of potential partners. And when you finally kiss Mr Right, you'll discover he's no longer your heart's desire.

You've got to be open to unexpected princeliness.

You'll also then come to see that the world isn't divided into frogs and frog-princes. It's all princes.

It's the random connections that generate wealth, not the targeted ones. Random connections *discover* wealth. The fifth, and final, key to being a good node is to *be open to random encounters.*

If you are open to random encounters, the principles of network economics will pervade your thoughts and actions, and influence all your behaviour. It's a very low-effort path to a massively enlarged and enriched world.

Key 5: Be open to random encounters.

Do The Strand

We started this chapter with the phrase *stranded at the top.* The word *strand* means a beach: London's famous Strand thoroughfare was originally the northern beach of the Thames. Our colloquial meaning of *stranded* refers to situations like Robinson Crusoe's: left on a beach, miles from civilisation, passed by no ships. Crusoe is ejected from his network, and survives with the help of his faith, his ingenuity – and the assistance of other networks that he barely recognises, in the cultures and ecology of his island.

But *strand* can take another meaning. A strand can also be a *thread.* A strand can connect two nodes, although tenuously. London's Strand evolved from a beach to a busy thoroughfare that connects the City with Westminster.

A strand can lead us through a labyrinth. And, when combined in a rope, strands make strong connectors.

I hold my Lunch Club events at Pizza Express in the Strand, to remind me that the little things we do as networkers add up to great effects.

We began this chapter with the concept of professional loneliness. We saw how being connected within networks removes the faulty point of view that leads to this kind of isolation.

Dispelling professional loneliness is simply a matter of replacing one meaning of stranded with another. Not left behind, but connected. Not shipwrecked, but lifelined.

All those links in our networks – the ties that make us what we are – are strands too. They're strands in the sense of storylines. Our links embody the interests we have in common, lay the foundations for our conversations and suggest directions for our explorations together. A vibrant, active network is like a mass of unfolding human stories, taking place in real time.

It's really the only place to be. It's where you belong. It's where you were always meant to be.

Networking is natural. Human beings are social animals, endlessly fascinated about each other, endlessly delighted at the infinite variety that we show in our deeds and our dreams. The concepts and keys in this chapter will return you to that natural state.

The Keys to Being a Good Node

1. Be aware that you are a node.

2. Take responsibility for all your communications.

3. Describe yourself in fifty words.

4. Maintain your link neighbourhood.

5. Be open to random encounters.

Chapter 3
Reach is a Verb

Conversations create transactions

This chapter is about shifting habits. It's concerned with how people traditionally spend their time in business, and how those habits don't transfer to the world of networking. I have a pop at business meetings – but since the main thrust of this book is that you need to have *lots* of meetings, it's only fair that I make it clear what *kind* of meetings I mean.

I also challenge fixed ideas about time and its relationship with money, because the substantial benefits of networking only come about when you become more flexible about how you invest your time, and when you enlarge your expectations about the rewards you want.

For those who are still unsure about the vital role of networking, I look at how networking is like insurance and, ultimately, a pension: an essential safety-net to ensure your professional and social well-being going forward. Finally, I look briefly at the kinds of new habits that networkers develop, so that you can start to change your behaviour today.

Force of Habit

The easiest thing to acquire, and the hardest to lose, is a habit. Some habits are beneficial – like looking both ways when we cross a road. Other habits are detrimental, and we spend large amounts of time, money and worry trying to eradicate them.

There's a set of habits that have a particularly bad effect on networking. These aren't personal habits. I don't teach people to behave in some "perfect" way – all you need to network is to be yourself.

I can't stress this enough. Networking is not acting. Networking is the real you.

The habits I'm referring to are those practices that we absorb in our working lives. They're the behaviours, protocols and superstitious dances that we learn working in organisations.

Making Better Meetings

Networking means having meetings – lots of meetings. I have over 1,000 meetings per year. But these are not the kind of meetings you may be familiar with in the corporate setting.

Anyone who has worked in an organisation of any size will be familiar with the huge number of meetings that have to be got through before any work can get done. In some organisations, meetings have taken the place of all other forms of work. Most of us know that if we can break the habit of calling (and attending) meetings, we can get more done.

And we all know that many of these meetings are more about Powerpoint and chocolate biscuits than anything else.

Ironically, if we go to fewer (yawn) meetings, we make time for more (wow!) meetings. By cutting down on work-substitute sessions, we can create space in our schedules for meaningful interactions.

But you have to be committed to networking if you're going to shift your attention from those traditional meetings to *real* meetings. You'll be meeting new people, and discussing new topics. That takes effort. Don't let your newly liberated time get swallowed up by those old non-meetings.

Coming off "meetings"

For every meeting that arises in your daily life, ask these questions:

- Can the work be done in another way?
- Is my presence really vital?
- How much is this meeting costing us?

Clocking Off

A less obvious habit that is formed inside corporations is what I call *seasonalism*. If you've worked for a publicly quoted company, you'll have been affected by the periodicity over which the business reports to the stock market. For US listed companies, this is quarterly. Even companies which report only twice yearly (as UK listed companies do) usually run management reports on a quarterly basis.

And of course most businesses are monitoring progress on monthly, weekly and daily timelines. The habit of looking for results that fit into a particular calendar can quickly ruin your business and your career. The simple fact is that life rarely presents opportunities according to any seasonal model. Where the buying cycles of a market are clearly seasonal, those factors will underpin the main movements and developments in its industry. But in all other cases, life is haphazard, with events occurring at random. If you try to spread your activity across the calendar to fit some kind of idealised shape, you will fail. Inevitably, you will have good periods and bad periods. If you ever hit your target, that's likely to be as much a matter of luck as judgement. Yet few people truly recognise the power and influence of luck, and what that means for the way you organise your activities.

For example, many folks set themselves up as independent consultants after working in corporations. They take their professional skills and experience to the market, unencumbered by a large-company mentality (all those meetings!) and free to serve their clients in the way they want. Yet most of these newly independent folks target themselves on a monthly horizon – right from the start.

It takes at least five years to establish most startups. Giving yourself a 30-day horizon is a good way of killing your chances of surviving and thriving. If you're starting a business, you need to be prepared for periods of lean and periods of fat.

This might mean saving up before you embark on your new life, or accepting the need to tighten your belt as you go along – or, more likely, both. Since five years is sixty months, you need enough money salted away to remove sixty months' pain, in the way of paying your bills. Once you've made these preparations, the monthly targets don't matter much.

Yes, you need to keep score. But it's more important that you don't put yourself under unnecessary pressures. You're only accountable to yourself, and your dependants. The concept of a month derives from the motion of the moon. What's that got to do with business? Your salary, and your bills, have habituated you to this antiquated business rhythm. If you let it go, your world will become much more flexible. It will be less predictable; the rewards will arrive haphazardly; but the rewards will be much greater. Some months I receive nothing, while at other times the money pours in.

The Time/Money Equation

A chronic extension of seasonalism is an over-developed sense that "time is money". It's true that ultimately time is the only thing you can turn into money, either by delivering services or developing products. But time is the only thing you have for doing *anything*.

Look at it this way. When you work for someone else, they take care of the building, the heating, the furniture and so on. The company takes all this clutter off your hands so you can get on with your job. Your job – anybody's job – is to keep turning your time into money.

When you work for yourself, you have to look after all that "non-essential" stuff too. You therefore have less time to turn into money. The fees you set for your services will reflect these overheads.

But wait a minute. Whether you work for a company or for yourself, you know that time doesn't convert into money in an *even* way. Salaries and accounting periods smooth out the creation of money from time, with predictable sums popping up at regular intervals.

But day by day, hour by hour, the relationship between time and money is a much bumpier ride.

You might spend a month on a project: yet the piece of work that generated the value may have taken a split-second. It might have been a great idea, or a helpful summarisation of a position, or a decisive intervention in a debate. But it took no time at all.

This principle applies in spades to networking. Remember all those frogs that are really princes? Even when we know that every frog is a prince, we can't generate benefit with every prince at the moment of kissing. We're still going to have a high kissing-to-marrying ratio. If we're filling in mental timesheets, it's going to look like we're wasting lots of time, and generating little money, especially if we discount the value of all the information we are gathering and sharing during this time.

With networking, the investment in time is constant and the rewards are intermittent and unpredictable.

This holds true for all kinds of businesses too, except for a rare handful in stable, commodity businesses (and they're getting rarer). Much of the larger company's infrastructure is there to insulate the shareholders from the haphazardness of its profits – and to create a sense of predictability for employees and customers alike. When you're networking, you get rid of the insulation, and embrace the unpredictability.

Attitudes to how time should be spent form the biggest barrier for people starting out as networkers. You can lose these attitudes by immersing yourself in the networking activity.

Turn your attention to the process itself, and soon you'll lose your anxiety about the clock and the calendar. (There's more about this in Chapter 8.)

Remember, when you network you're not going to be punished for relaxing the "rules" you learned in the corporate setting. Those rules don't transfer to networking. And you're not accountable to an authority figure when you network. You're responsible to your network – and that's quite a different thing. It's also a responsibility that keeps on growing along with the increasing size of your network. When your network reaches 20,000 people in 120 countries, as the Ecademy network did around Month 51, you'll see that networking creates responsibilities far greater than anyone could ever hand you as a traditional employee.

Networking as Insurance

It might sound like I've unpicked all the traditional trappings of business practice, and left you with little to go on! But as you'll see, this book is about providing you with habits and techniques that replace these unhelpful habits.

But before we move on to the new habits, I want to make one connection with a traditional area of business – one that reflects our most conservative and cautious attitudes.

This is the business of insurance. Insurance exists to protect us against the unforeseen. We pay premiums regularly as insurance against a rare event. The rare event might be serious illness, or loss of property.

We do not begrudge our regular payments for not delivering us immediate benefits. In fact, we continue to hope that we won't need to invoke our policies even as we maintain the payments on them. We use insurance as a rational means of safeguarding our future.

Networking is a form of insurance. In fact, your network is your *cover*.

Your network is what will protect you from some rainy day in the future. It is the safety net that will catch you if you fall from grace. Your network is an asset that you build and nourish in case you need it. It's the most important thing you can build over your lifetime, next to your health and your family.

And – guess what – your network is also a source of mental well-being and fellowship, so it's not that far removed from your health and family anyway.

And just like insurance, networks need maintaining over the long term. You can't insure for an event *after* it's happened. Confucius said: "Don't wait until you are thirsty to dig a well!"

It's the same with networking. Do it while you don't need it. Do it all the time.

If you treat networking in this way, you'll also be building an emotional and financial pension for the day when you don't feel like working so hard. By building and nurturing your network, you create a shared store of goodwill that you can draw on in later life. The relationships you build during your more pro-active years act as an investment for later life, ensuring that you can call on shared interests and memories when you have the greatest time to enjoy them to the full.

This is why habits are so important to successful networking. You need to make networking an aspect of everything you do. It needs to be a constant part of your life. A network isn't just for Christmas, it's for life.

Reach for the New Habit

Resolve to acquire a new habit: Reaching out to people.

Reach is a verb. That means it's something you *do*.

When it's used as a noun, "reach" is a *thing*. In our terms, your reach might be the extent of your network neighbourhood. Though really, when you network effectively, your reach is limitless. By following the links, you can make your way to virtually anyone. (We'll see how this works later, when we look at the new maths of networking.)

But "reach" is also a verb. That means it's something you *do*. This is a much more important use of the word. I want you to forget about "reach" as a measurement, and start thinking of it as a compulsive habit instead. Look for people to connect with. Start seeing people that come into your orbit as people you can connect with. Make the first move – you'll be surprised how quickly people will respond to your gesture. And you'll be pleased with the warmth you receive.

Clearly, you've got to act within the bounds of accepted behaviour in your culture and surroundings. But don't be afraid to sail near the edge of those bounds.

In the USA, it's acceptable to talk to just about anyone, even if he's a total stranger. But you shouldn't be surprised if that person drifts away without saying goodbye. In the UK, it's traditionally hard to get to know people. It's not quite that we need our parents to know their parents, or that we have to be wearing the same football team's jersey.

But we need to pick on a potential item of current interest rather than start a conversation at random. (That must be why we love to talk about the weather.)

Luckily, as the power of networking grows, safe venues are opening up where people can be more upfront about creating new relationships. Ecademy's networking events are billed as networking events. Even the shyest attendee knows that the point of the event is to meet and talk with other people, so we all forgive each other any clumsy starts. And by using the Fifty Words technique, networkers signal their interest in instant engagement, and in finding common ground with each other in less than a minute.

It's also significant that Ecademy's online dimension lets people get to know each other before they ever meet in "real life". Members can find each other, and find out about each other, via email or instant messaging, and by reading each other's profiles and contributions. They can also be recommended to each other by contacts they have in common. And they can find new contacts by joining clubs organised around their personal interests. Within eight weeks of the launch of Ecademy's Club feature, 185 clubs had been born.

Outside of the safe venues, you can give yourself a head start in networking by excusing your own ice-breakers. Don't task yourself with being the smoothest conversation-opener in the world. It's not a competition. You're not being marked on the brilliance of your opening.

Above all, be aware that people want to be reached. If it's a business setting, you can be sure that any effort you make to reach someone will spark some response. (Although everyone has their off-days: please don't punch the occasional non-player.)

What about less obvious settings? Can you introduce yourself to people in shops, on the beach, in the street? If you have a genuine item of shared interest to communicate, and if your second sense tells you the other person wants to be reached, then go for it. Great businesses have flowered from chance observations made at the race track, or business cards swapped by drivers in a traffic jam. It happens!

Get in the habit of reaching. Make reaching your default behaviour. You'll then be checking with yourself to see if you *shouldn't* make an approach, rather than wondering if you should. It's the actions that you're consciously aware of that drive your behaviour. So if you're consciously trying to reach, you'll reach more people. The more people you reach, the better your sense of appropriate reaching behaviour will be. The more fun it'll be.

As E.M. Forster wrote at the beginning of his novel *Howards End*: Only Connect. Forster believed in the supreme power of human relationships, and put the struggle to connect at the heart of all his writings. That impulse, and that power, is with us all, and it underwrites all our actions, however much they get obscured. All of our life is a reaching.

Safe openers

Here are some simple opening statements that you can use to start conversations:

- How do you know ...? (the host)

- It's busy, isn't it?

- Am I in the right room? (Unusual, but it works.)

- What's the wine like?

- How did you travel here?

- Who introduced you to this network?

Business Flirting?

Is the reaching I'm describing a kind of business flirting? I guess it is. You're advertising that you're available, interested, looking for a connection.

But with networking you can have many more committed relationships than would be manageable (or possibly legal) in the world of romance. Networkers share themselves.

This isn't about promiscuity. That would imply you were making some kind of transaction with everyone you meet. And I specifically advise you *not* to regard networking as a matter of transactions. Transactions deliver value that we can convert into food and drink, but they are a by-product of networking. (You can fill in the analogy between love and sex.)

And although I'm promoting relationships – because networks are collections of relationships – I actually advise you to focus on something less than relationships: *Conversations.*

Conversations are what actually happen during networking. They are the energy that is generated and consumed in personal interactions. Human beings thrive on conversations as a vital energy source for recharging our batteries. Conversations are where we truly meet. And *conversations create transactions.*

I don't mean that each conversation creates one transaction. That's not the way the maths works. It's more likely that one transaction will be created from a mass of conversations. (But, as we shall see later, the value of that one transaction can be substantial.) And, very occasionally, a single conversation creates a mass of transactions: social, professional, emotional, informational, spiritual and yes, sometimes financial ones.

People Sell People

You've probably heard the saying *People buy people.* There's more than a grain of truth in it. I might persuade myself that I've bought a product because of my great need for it, because of its great features, or because of its fabulous value for money.

Behind that justification there's a person or a bunch of people. There might be the person who first told me about the product (perhaps a trusted colleague), or an actual sales person who demonstrated the product to me.

I might have bought the product because I admire the brand; in which case, I'm buying the people who are represented by the brand. I want to be like them. (Oobe-doo, to quote the *Jungle Book* song again!)

Now, if people buy people, then it had better hold true that *people sell people* too. If they don't, then no transactions ever take place.

Does that sound terrible? Does the idea of selling yourself, or selling someone else, sound like a wicked act?

All communication is selling. When we speak, we want to convey an idea from our mind to the other person's mind. And we want them to transfer their ideas to us. We buy each other. In a healthy networking conversation, it's impossible to say who's selling and who's buying. The direction of flow changes all the time.

Most importantly, networkers do not focus on "closing". If anything, they're obsessed with "opening". They want to learn as much as possible. They want to explore as widely as possible. They want to unearth as many possibilities – for all the parties in the encounter – as they can.

When I connect with people inside Ecademy, I ask them who I can connect them with. But I also network with people who aren't (yet!) members of Ecademy. I often find people who have written compelling articles, or made inspiring remarks in a business meeting.

I often reach out to them by suggesting that they get a larger audience for their message – and high quality feedback – by posting it in one of Ecademy's forums. In this way, Ecademy becomes a way of initiating conversations wherever I go. I'm giving something, because I'm offering a low-effort, high-reward route to wider exposure for the thinkers and communicators I meet.

So, although networkers sell themselves, and are enthusiastic buyers of others, they are not anxious about outcomes. They do "work the room", but it's not work. It just comes naturally – because, to habitual networkers, it is natural to be interested in other people, and to reach out to them.

They try to be in the place, the moment, the group. They are fully alive to the situation, excited by its possibilities, but calm about their own role.

Externals such as goals, achievements and status cannot satisfy our internal needs. Being with people can help us be ourselves. In the final analysis, this is networking's great gift to the modern world. The rest – the enhanced businesses, the newly created opportunities – is just icing.

Chapter 4

Me, You and the New Maths

Your standard of living is directly related to the size of your network.

In this chapter I lay out what it's like to be a Power Networker. There's a little mathematics in this chapter, but it's not the scary sort. There are no Greek symbols and you won't need a slide rule (not even to keep your eyelids from closing, I promise).

I also turn the spotlight on you, and what you can bring to networking. Networks are meaningless without nodes, and you are an important node.

I ask whether networking is a fad, and whether it's something you can succeed with as a dabbler. ("No" and "No!", in that order.) Then there's a bit more maths, in which we look at the simple, inexorable power of randomness – and the best way of spotting talent in a monkey.

Finally, I look at how networking is engrained in my life, and why it should be in yours.

Being Me

Let's look at the realities of being a Power Networker. What's it like being me – someone who lives by networking, and who lives *for* networking?

Well, it's fantastic being me. I'm immensely wealthy and fabulously handsome. I can defy gravity and, if I'm in the mood, stop time. I get my kicks rubbing shoulders with celebrities – when I'm not sunning myself in some exclusive resort. Because I'm a prominent networker, I never have to work, or worry.

Let's rewind that section and have another shot…

The truth is, I don't have a Ferrari on each foot. What I have is a thousand meetings per year. That's one *thousand* meetings, each and every year.

In 2002, I took more than 1,300 meetings. In the same year, I won 25 pieces of business. That's a 'success rate' of 1.9%.

But wait a minute: my success rate isn't balanced. It's *skewed*. And it's skewed towards overwhelming benefits.

Here's how it works. On the basis of 2002's figures, 98.1% of my meetings don't lead directly to any income. On the profit and loss sheet of life, they add up to lost time. All those minutes, all those hours, have been consumed, and they're not coming back again. Imagine that I value my time at one pound per minute. That means every 100 minutes, I notionally lose £98.10.

No one likes to lose money – even notional money. And, strange creatures that we are, we mourn losses of money in a disproportionate way. It hurts us as much to lose twenty pence in a faulty parking meter as it does to lose a tenner on a horse. Small losses exact a massive emotional toll.

However: when I win, in my 1.9% window, I win big. Each minute of my time in the 1.9% window is worth much more than a pound. In 2002, my 1.9% 'success' window created £750,000 for Ecademy.

That's what I call a skewed return. Networking always delivers returns that are skewed towards large, but rare, rewards. The economic result is all upside. The downside is in the emotional toll of all those many, tiny, disappointments.

I have found no other way to win from networking other than by going for *volume* and *variety*. I meet a lot of people, and they come from all walks of life. I need volume and variety to deliver my skewed return.

Let's introduce a very simple, and memorable, formula. Your network needs to contain 1,000 people for every £100,000 you want to earn.

Did you get that? Here it comes again: Your network needs to contain 1,000 people for every £100,000 you want to earn.

I think I can just see the head of that nail sticking out... Let's hammer it one more time. *Your network needs to contain 1,000 people for every £100,000 you want to earn.*

Being me means adjusting to this new maths.

People deficit

- How much money do you want to earn this year?

- How many people do you need in your network to earn your goal?

- How many people short are you?

Forget the "asset-rich, time-poor" label you may have heard. We're all people-poor, and that's the indicator that counts.

The New Maths

Researchers are beginning to discover something weird. The scale and disruptiveness of this discovery reminds me of the excitement that surrounded the emergence of complexity theory a decade or more ago. The discovery is: *Random connections are more potent than non-random connections.*

In the business context, this translates to the following law: *Random connections make more money than non-random ones.*

The corollary to this law is this: *Your standard of living is directly related to the size of your network.*

In 1998, I had 300 people in my network. At the time of writing, it stands at 20,000, 4,000 of whom I have met in "real life". During that period, my standard of living has tripled.

I'm not going to rehearse the detailed maths that's emerging now around randomness. Generally speaking, I don't talk too much about the maths. I *live* the maths. I play the ultimate numbers game.

I have at least a thousand *meetings* per year. Couldn't I have fewer meetings, but just *meet* the right people? Can't I just kiss the frogs who are princes?

I don't believe that anyone *meets* the right people. You can only *bump into* "right people". So, what you need to do is to generate more bumpingintoness. You need to speed up serendipity. Ecademy is a machine for manufacturing randomness, and accelerating serendipity.

Being You

I hope I've got across the fact that I'm a normal human being, albeit one who has a passionate interest in networking. I'm human and I bleed, like anyone else. One of the peculiar effects of leading Ecademy is that I make myself a target – a screen on which people project their needs and fears, and a basin into which they direct great volumes of both abuse and praise.

I mention this not because I want your sympathy, but because I want you to embrace the same leadership role. I want you to become a Power Networker, and to lead your own Ecademy Clubs. Remember that every "top" is a node? Well, every node is a top too. When you network – *seriously* network – you opt for a position of prominence in a community of your own choosing. You draw people to you. And some of those people will want you as their whipping boy.

Believe me, I'm whipped daily in many of the 500 or more emails I now receive every day.

Some of those people will believe that you really do have a Ferrari on each foot – when, like everyone else, you might just have do-do on your shoe.

Specifically, my vision for Ecademy is of a thriving community of networkers in every major population centre across the planet. An Ecademy thriving in every city, each drawing 10,000 members who help each other, spar with each other and enjoy life's journey with each other. My goal for Ecademy is 10,000 members in each of a thousand cities by 2050. That's ten million members.

And that means I need a Thomas in every city. We can replicate the software version of Thomas Power, the functions and features embodied in the Ecademy platform that we'll explore later – that's not a problem. But I'm not putting myself up for cloning. And even if it were possible and desirable, cloning would miss the point... Because Ecademy needs diversity in its leaders, just as it does in its network. It needs randomness in every dimension of its activities. It needs you.

Ecademy's future needs you to take the local lead, in your geographical area and in your areas of personal interest. I can't be everywhere at once, and I can't be anyone else but me. We need to populate this network with living, breathing, squabbling, laughing, learning individuals. People who are the masters of their own domains, and who recognise the additional power that is generated when domains become linked.

People who want to foster stronger ties in their local communities. People who are dedicated to reaching out to others.

You don't have to be ten feet tall. You don't need a black belt in winning friends and influencing people. All you need is a substantial measure of commitment. You need the mental and physical stamina to take 1,000 meetings per year. Ecademy has the tools and experience to support you in whatever way you want to extend and enrich the network. As you'll see in Chapter 5, our platform lets you create Clubs and Special Interest Groups, publish your own ideas and discuss the ideas of others, connect yourself and other people together via common interests... When it comes to a supportive environment for networking, I believe we've built the richest the world has ever seen – and we never stop making it better.

But however good the technology gets, and no matter how many Ecademists lead the way with must-join Clubs or must-read articles or must-go local events, Ecademy still needs more creative, committed individuals to breathe yet more life into the network.

That's you.

Give and take

You already know that networking is a two-way process, and that you should strive to give rather than take. But the maths of networking can also be expressed simply in terms of "gives" and "takes". It's the relationship between what you put out, and what you get back.

This is how it works:

- Forty-nine Gives result in one Take.

- If you have 1,000 meetings per year, you'll score 980 Gives and 20 Takes.

- Those twenty Takes will provide £100,000 in income.

The January Jogger

Have you seen the January Jogger? Perhaps you *are* a January Jogger. The new year arrives and with it a list of brave resolutions. You're going to take up that diet, give up that bad habit. Gym memberships shoot up in January – but by mid February it's possible to do your workout in peace as the January crowd thins out. When spring arrives, most of us have long lapsed back into our old ways.

At the start of 2003, Ecademy experienced a rapid acceleration in new members. At the same time, a number of new networking tools arrived on the scene and quickly garnered large (though possibly passive) memberships. Our January event in London topped out at more than 300 people. The walls of the venue bulged.

Why is networking suddenly fashionable? Why has the maths of networking become sexy? And why are people from every walk of life committing to becoming networkers? Are they January Joggers – or are they here for the long run?

Networking is a kind of insurance. I buy insurance to cover my house, my possessions and above all the health and prosperity of my family. Networking is *income insurance*. It is also *employability insurance*, and, I believe, *emotional health insurance* and *spiritual insurance*.

Some people take up networking and are in a great rush to see dividends. They see time spent on networking as an investment of their time, and they want a quick return. They may be anxious that they are about to be "let go" or downsized by their employers, and believe that networking is a way of attracting lifeboats.

Unfortunately, by the time you've lost your job, it's too late to start networking. You can't network effectively when you desperately need something from everyone you meet. You can only network well from an attitude of abundance, and with a cultivated disinterest in the outcome of any encounter. Care about the meeting, but don't get hung up on what the meeting has to produce for you. And collect those batches of fifty words we talked about in Chapter 2.

You need to be networking *all* the time, not just when you're hungry and think the networking goose could handily produce a golden egg. You pay your health insurance premiums every month that you *aren't* sick. Networking is no different: you pay your premiums by making your 1,000 meetings.

Some people take up networking not because they are worried about losing their jobs, but because they want to change their career direction.

For these folks, getting involved in some intensive networking can help them appreciate the huge variety of ways in which people earn their living, create worthwhile businesses and contribute to the evolving richness of our world.

But if they leave it at that, these people will not derive great benefits from their networks. They'll be browsing, but not contributing. They'll draw a little power from the network – don't worry, we've plenty left and we're generating it all the time – but they won't hang around long enough to find the real energy. That's because they're using networking as a way of reflecting, rather than growing.

There's nothing wrong with reflection, and I also use my networks to learn about other people and their interests, passions and goals.

But I try to remember that the network is a living, organic, fluid entity that must be participated in to be truly understood. It's not meant to be a mirror. It's not there to tell me how I should behave, or what I should strive to become. It's a source of new questions, rather than a collection of answers.

Does networking only work if you do it all the time? I suppose that running in January is, for most people, better than taking no exercise at all. But I think that running *because* it's January is a poor way of organising your life. If only it were also true that a little networking never did anyone any harm.

Unfortunately, I find that people who dabble in networking – because it's fashionable, or because they're looking for a job – get little benefit, and even come away from the experience with an anti-networking frame of mind. That's because the new maths of networking demands that you do lots of it. And the only way to do lots of networking is to integrate it into your life.

Lucky Fools

I'm indebted to Nassim Nicholas Taleb for his quirky, personal and truly compelling book *Fooled by Randomness*. Taleb is a derivatives trader, and he uses the maths of skewed returns to organise his business. In the book, he shows how people commonly mistake *luck* for *skill*, and how this misleads their judgements.

Think of it this way. (Taleb doesn't use this example, but I hope it will resonate for a British audience.) One of your distant ancestors helps the king off his horse. The king is in a particularly good mood, because he won the battle today. He decides to make your ancestor a lord.

Several centuries later, you find yourself born to a position where you are asked to rule on issues as diverse as the building of a new airport, the education of the nation's children, and whether or not your own power should be removed. Whether this is good luck or bad luck, it's luck.

It's not to say that a hereditary peer automatically has no skills. But he owes his *position* to luck, not skill.

Taleb points out that a *survivor principle* operates in life. If you start out with a large number of people, and you winnow them in successive generations, there will be a surviving population who have been "selected" at random.

It's like the story about the infinite number of monkeys, all hammering away at typewriters. An infinite number of monkeys will one day produce a masterpiece. But that miraculous monkey is very unlikely to repeat his performance. He has been lucky, not skilful. If, on the other hand, you start with ten monkeys and one of them writes *Hamlet* within a week – hire the monkey. That's likely to be skill, not luck.

"Lucky Fools" is the name Taleb gives to survivors. Filmmaker Woody Allen said that "eighty percent of success is showing up". When Britain's National Lottery was born a few years ago (following a century when government-backed lotteries were outlawed as immoral influences on the poor), one newspaper published a list of "top tips" for playing the lottery. The number one tip was: "Buy a ticket! You've got to be in it to win it."

I use the power of networking to compete with Lucky Fools. I use networking to generate a huge wealth of opportunity that can match, or beat, the inherited advantage of the unskilled, but well positioned, survivor.

When I left home, I didn't leave with money. I left with love. I was propelled into the wider world with the love of my family behind me, and a belief that a love of people is the foundation of life.

Networking is...

- Knowledge

- Richness

- Family

- Wealth

- Travel

- Friendship

- Success

- Peace

- Love

- Life

Everyone, Everywhere

You'll notice that I combine two levels of attitude to networking. I see it as an economic activity, governed by the maths of networking. At the same time, I see it as an expression of our fundamental need for meaningful relationships.

I don't think there's any contradiction between these two takes on networking. They're equally valid. And they both work.

My networking is both "shallow", if you like, in the sense that it's about volume and variety, and "deep", in that it's about genuinely connecting with people. I'm sometimes criticised for my use of network mathematics: it can strike people as simplistic and cynical.

But at the same time, I'm criticised for my supposed naivety in believing in the power of genuine human relationships.

To me, both these criticisms miss the point. Network mathematics is an objective fact, and a completely neutral force. It makes about as much sense to push against network mathematics as it does to question the validity of gravity when something heavy is about to land on your head. The vital importance of human relationships is also a simple fact. Failure to stroke baby human beings causes them to die. We never lose this need for each other's love, and we can never have our fill.

I think about how networking might look to people who don't practise it, because I want to bring those people into the networked world. I won't accept an antipathy to networking as a reason to avoid networking with someone! If anything, an anti-networking attitude will just spur me on. I believe that networking runs through us all as an instinct, and denying its presence is about as useful as saying you don't need food and drink.

As a result, networking is integrated into every aspect of my life. There is no line where "the networker" ends and "the person" begins. Networking is my life. Networking happens at work, at school, at home and on holiday.

I network with suppliers, clients, staff, shareholders, family, friends and the people I bump into. What they see is what they get.

Networking is the real Thomas Power, and it's the real you. Networking doesn't come out of a bottle, like fake tan. It's not a veneer. It's not an act.

My approach to networking has evolved during more than twenty years, and more than 20,000 meetings with all kinds of people from all walks of life, with all kinds of goals. The mechanics of networking centre on asking questions, listening, making notes, reviewing your notes and pondering their significance. If you do all these things, and do them as part of your daily life, and enjoy doing them, you're a networker. That's all there is to being me, or being you.

Chapter 5

A Platform for Networking

I am a software (and so are you)

This chapter is about the tools you can use to make yourself an efficient and effective networker. There's a lot of information to manage when you network: contacts, conversations, link words.

I also present in this chapter a glimpse of how I use the Ecademy website – the software version of me and the other Power Networkers who have influenced its development.

No one knows better than I do that our time is limited. Unless I can find some way of slowing down the earth's spin, the day will always be about 24 hours long. Can I physically, logistically, *humanly* do more than 1,000 meetings per year? Will my meetings index peak at the 1,300 I managed in 2002?

What I need is some way that I can increase both the volume and the variety of the meetings I have. At Ecademy, we've developed the approach and the tools to do just that. This chapter will show you how to get the best out of them.

The Essential Tools

Member Directory

Naturally, you're going to need a secure and handy place where you can keep contact details of all the people you meet.

An electronic diary that you can carry around and synchronise with your desktop computer is a useful tool. One of the popular Palm or PocketPC models will do the trick, as will an increasing number of mobile phones. With a pocket device synchronised with your PC, you can do the heavy typing and analysis work at your desk, but never be without your valuable contacts database when you're on the move. Some pocket computers, or PDAs (Personal Digital Assistants) are smart enough to dial your mobile phone for you when you select a contact. And all of them let you "beam" your own business card details to another user in the room.

Another cool gadget that's worth thinking about is a business card reader from www.cardscan.com. These neat machines scan ordinary business cards, convert the printing on them into computer-readable text, and store the details on your computer.

The Member Directory at Ecademy.com contains the usual name and address details, plus phone, email and instant messaging addresses. It also contains a section for the member's fifty words, plus an area the member can fill with their own text. Members can also upload their photograph to the Directory.

Messaging Systems

You know about SMS (texting), but are you using it effectively in your networking activity? Texting is a great way of keeping in touch with contacts, and letting them have small snippets of news. But only use it when you have something genuinely useful to say, or you'll start to lose friends.

You also need to be a smart and sensitive user of email. Emails to new contacts need to be short, courteous – and useful. Be interesting. Tell your contact something they need to know about their company, their industry, or one of their interests. Be one of their allies in the information storm, directing valuable items to their attention.

Even better – connect them. Match your contacts with other people that they need to know. This way, you'll be adding value to your network by increasing the number of connections within it. The more paths, the more value – because the money's in the links, not the nodes.

Various wireless email systems now enable us to use email in a highly reactive, "always-on" way. Email is becoming more like texting – except that fewer people are equipped for wireless email than are used to texting. People who respond to emails from their BlackBerry devices speak volumes about their care for their correspondents. They show that they'll interrupt whatever they're doing to respond to a friendly email. You can be one of these highly available people.

The last type of messaging system that's in common use is Instant Messaging (IM). IM exists in several incompatible flavours, with the leading applications coming from Microsoft, Yahoo! and AOL. These systems allow people to chat in text online. They also support emoticons – that's smiley faces, to you and me. Open Source products like Jabber and Trillian allow you to chat with other people regardless of which IM program they are using.

Email, texting and Instant Messaging are beginning to converge, and the next few years will see continued uptake of real-time messaging capabilities. These facilities are a boon for networkers. Not only can you reach people by voice; you can also pop textual messages into their consciousnesses, allowing them to deal with them in their own time.

Badges

It's rarely thought of as a networking tool, but have you thought of having a name badge made for yourself? They don't cost much, they last forever, and they're guaranteed to spell your name correctly. I don't like pinning cardboard badges on my clothes, and sticky labels seem to float off me. (And there was I thinking I had a magnetic personality.) My own badge is a much better solution.

My badge has also saved me in situations where people are clustered together without identification. Obviously, you're not going to pin a badge on yourself at the airport terminal and start glad-handing people. But if you're at an event where people are supposed to mix, say between presentation sessions or over lunch, then there's no harm in wearing your name with pride.

At the very least, you'll be giving yourself an opener: "I brought my own badge!"

Tools inventory

- What tools do you use for capturing contact details?

- Can you describe a contact in the depth you need to network with her fully?

- Do you use email, text and Instant Messaging as low-pressure, high-value channels for keeping in touch with your network?

- How often do you search consciously for items of information that might help members of your network?

Spinning Your Web

Once you're equipped with the essential tools, you're well-placed to start gathering masses of data on your networking travels. But what do you do with all that data?

The first thing you'll want to do is to relate the people in your network somehow. There will be many ways you want to do this, so you'll have to use a database. For example, you might want to relate people by their geographical location, the line of work they are in, or when you last talked with them. All of these items need to be searchable attributes in your database. I would also add attributes for link words, and for people who might be usefully introduced to each other.

Recording relationships amongst people can become complicated. It's easy enough to see that two or more people in your network work for the same company. But it's harder to figure out where they fit in their company's organisational structure – let alone what common projects they might be working on, or have an influence on.

Your personal network map is also going to be necessarily limited by the people you can find to add to it. Using an online networking platform such as Ecademy gives you access to a wide community of people who are just itching to be better connected. You can therefore use the platform to grow your network, as well as to store it.

The Platform

When talking about Ecademy's systems (or "platform", as we call it), I sometimes say: *I am a software.*

There are two things going on with this statement. One is by the bye, but interesting nonetheless: it's that I use the term "software" as if it were a common noun – as if "softwares" were animals, and we could individuate them. (And why not? Don't you think software has become a species?)

The second layer to this statement is that, through the genius of Julian Bond and Glenn Watkins (who write the 1's and 0's that make up our platform), my networking beliefs, habits and support needs have been realised in software. It's as if someone has made a movie, or a computer game, out of my life (but much less scary).

The Ecademy platform was built initially as a direct consequence of how I go about networking, and what I felt would help me achieve more as a networker. As the platform has grown and other networkers have started to use it, the software has begun to become more like them too. The platform mimics the practices of committed networkers. It's an aggregation of the memories and behaviour of an army of networkers. That's why it looks, and acts, like nothing else you've touched.

Using the Ecademy Website

This is how I use the Ecademy website in my networking activities. Let me take you through a typical session.

Firstly, I check the site's Alexa ranking. Alexa (www.alexa.com) ranks websites according to the number of people using them. A user who installs the Alexa toolbar feeds his website usage back to the company, which then aggregates the data with behaviour patterns from millions of other users. Alexa isn't a perfect measure of website popularity, but it's the best that we have. The Alexa technology also fits well with the kind of user we have at Ecademy. Ecademy isn't primarily a resource for people who want to look up a fact or download a specific item, so it doesn't need to appear at the top of any standard search engine result set. Ecademy exists to connect people, so I measure its standing in the community by its popularity amongst connected users. Alexa also tells me how Ecademy's traffic pattern is developing over time, graphing the raw statistics and calculating averages over different periods. I make sure that the trends across all Alexa measures continue to be positive.

After I've absorbed the Ecademy ranking on Alexa, I check the site's basic statistics. These include the raw page view numbers, and the number of new members. I also track the number of Power Networkers, and the sources of our inbound clicks. Few of our hits come from passive page links at other sites, since we grow by personal recommendation. The majority of our traffic is generated by returning members rather than random visitors. But it's always interesting to see who's pointing to Ecademy from their sites.

By now I'm itching to check the reputation statistics. I look to see who's top for content contribution, and who has the biggest network. I aim to stay at the top of the charts. I confess I rarely make Number One in the content chart, but I'm always in the top five. And I fight as hard as I can to retain my spot as top networker.

But I look forward to the day I'm toppled. When I can't hold on to the top spot, I'll know that Ecademy has really exploded. This thing has to be bigger than me – but I'll keep on struggling to stay in the lead. Why? That way I keep the bar shifting. That way the network keeps growing beyond even my dreams.

I then look at the top page views. This gives me a sense of what Ecademists rate as the important issues of the day. I get an immediate picture of where people are putting their conversational effort, what the hot topics are, and who the provocateurs and clarifiers are. It's a quick way of keying into the spirit of the community, and a bit like walking through the virtual halls of Ecademy, listening to snippets of conversation and noticing where the laughter is coming from, and where the deep discussions are taking place.

Now it's time to look in depth at how I'm performing as a networker within the community. I click across to my own page hits, to see who's been looking at my profile. This is one of the most powerful features of Ecademy. We let Power Networkers see who's been dropping by their profile page, so that they can judge the impact they're having and change their behaviour appropriately. I can often tell why people are visiting my profile page. Often it's as a direct result of my reaching out to a member via email.

Sometimes people visit my profile page in response to a blog I posted. What's a blog? The word is a shortened version of "weblog". (That's how you make a new word these days: jam two old ones together, then hack some bits off.) A blog is a kind of online diary. Individual entries have come to be known as blogs too, although the more correct name is "post" or "posting". Blogging software allows people to write their own web content and publish it instantly, without fiddling around with difficult tools or (horror of horrors) actual code. Bloggers write their posts on a web form, click on the "publish" icon, and their thoughts are made available for the world to see. Ecademy's blogging software gives every member their own blog, allows members to search for terms across all the blogs, and puts links to the most recent postings on the Ecademy home page. Your blog can include links to other material, wherever it is on the web, as well as pictures.

Any visitor to my profile page who is "blue" – that is, she is keyed with a blue or "not yet connected" symbol – is guaranteed a prompt email from me.

And I offer them something in my email. I often ask: "Who can I connect you with?" It stands to reason that as a committed networker I should be able to make my network work for others. You might want to make other offers, of course. The crucial thing is that you reach out.

Now I review my network. I have a simple rule for managing my network: I won't have any blues. I look at my UK and non-UK network to ensure that there are no blues in either.

I play the networking functionality like a game. For example, one wily member regularly deletes me from his network every time I contact him. I hear nothing but good things about this guy, but he shoots me down every time because he's keeping his network below ten members so that he doesn't have to become a Power Networker! Now that's intriguing behaviour – and I have an appetite for intriguing behaviour. I wonder if he can achieve his goals within this constraint? I know – I'll send him an email now and ask him…

Next I look at which blogs are getting the most attention from members. This is a good way of determining the rising stars in the network, and of spotting those members whose primary way of establishing their profile is to contribute content.

Your choice

You might use the Ecademy platform in an entirely different way. I know some Ecademists who follow the blogs, and then contact the bloggers who interest them most. These people tend to be ideas-driven.

I know other Ecademists who post unusual or contentious items to their blogs, then check to see who is intrigued enough to visit their profile pages as a result. These people are more like fishermen.

I know other people who make straight for the member directory on a regular basis and look to see which recent joiners live in their neighbourhood, or work in their field, or even just have an interesting job title.

Whatever platform you use for your networking, make sure you do invest in some support. If you're going to go for volume and diversity, and keep track of all those developing conversations that create transactions, you need some way of managing the process. The back of an envelope isn't going to do the job.

Clubbing

People have been clubbing for much longer than dance music has been around. The older generation of politicians used to talk about who amongst them was "clubbable", and they didn't mean that they were off to Ibiza at the weekend (or that they should be beaten over the head). They were really alluding to how much someone networked.

The celebrated diarist Samuel Pepys, a Power Networker if ever there was one, recorded how he went "clubbing" in the London of the 1660s. The young Pepys made little distinction between the relationships he made at work, in the family, or amongst the people he met by chance in the tumultuous age he lived in. And London's clubs – its talking shops – were one of the means he used to network.

Clubs have been reborn on the Ecademy platform. In early 2003, we responded to members' demands for a further level of organisation on the site by giving them the facility to create areas of interest, and to recruit members to those areas. At least, that's what we *thought* we were doing. As it rapidly became clear, what we'd actually done was to add an entirely new dimension not only to the way Ecademy is organised, but also to the way people perceive and exploit Ecademy.

Ecademy's Clubs are your opportunity to build your own networks and grow your own businesses around those networks.

These networks don't have to be business networks. They can equally be social networks, friendship networks or e-learning networks. They can be networks for finance directors, debating networks, educational networks, art networks, engineering networks, design networks, travel networks, holiday networks, skiing networks or working mother networks. The list is endless.

An astonishing 185 Clubs were formed within the first two months of our launching the service. Clubs are knowledge networks. They are places you can go to learn, to network and to develop your career. We don't limit the size, shape, scope or scale of these networks. Clubs find their own directions and destinies. They're a direct expression of the life that networks take on. Clubs emerge as organising principles, and centres of energy, within the seething activity of the Ecademy network as a whole.

I believe that the Clubs show our determination to enable the largest, strongest and most diverse network on the planet. They demonstrate how, far from having all the answers, the founders of Ecademy cannot predict the evolution of the network. The birth and flourishing of the different Clubs that we see appearing daily prove the vitality of the networking principle. Networking is irrepressible. You can't keep it down.

Starting a Club isn't something you do lightly. Leading a Club makes you a leader in the networked world. It gives you a position of prominence. It also increases your responsibilities.

The responsibilities you have as a good node, such as maintaining your link neighbourhood, are magnified when you start a Club. So you have to be up for it.

So when you consider your Club think carefully about the name of that Club and what you want the Club to do or represent. The most popular of Ecademy's first wave of Clubs was Donato Esposito's Gadgets R Us Club. The name tells you that this Club is meant to be fun. It also says something about the techie element of our membership.

Author, consultant and part-time 1970s singing sensation Mike Southon built his Beermat Club around his book The Beermat Entrepreneur (written with Chris West), his speaking engagements, his consulting services, his band (Mike Fab-Gere and the Permissive Society) and his lifestyle. Different as Mike and I are, his Club echoes many of the founding themes of Ecademy.

I started Ecademy around my books, my speaking, my globetrotting and my research for the books.

I'd always wanted a place where could I meet the readers of my books, listen to a broad range of opinion, and travel the world searching for new points of view. I also dreamed of a place where I could share concepts for new books with like minds. I wanted a place I could go to each month and meet people, hear a speaker, laugh, have fun and go home emotionally uplifted. To me, Ecademy has always been like a private club in a box.

Ecademy Clubs let you build your own network place in your own image. So in order to create your Club, you need to ask yourself: What is Ecademy to me?

Is Ecademy a place you hope to find contacts? A place to find friends? Perhaps you hope to find a partner. We can point to one wedding from Ecademy's first fifty months.

Maybe Ecademy is a place you hope will boost your business? Or a place you go to share your thoughts or test your ideas? It could be a place you go to socialise and get away from the crazed pace of the world we live in – a place of rest and therapy without any hidden agendas. These are the meanings that should determine the nature of your Club.

When you've decided what your Club will be, and what it will be called, it's simple to create it on the Ecademy site. Once your Club is in place it's time to invite your peers, friends, clients, prospects, suppliers, shareholders, employees, brother or sister to join.

There's a simple "Invite" button that lets you welcome them in.

You then need to drive debate, answer points raised in discussions and keep pushing your group along. That's a lot of work in itself – but it isn't enough.

People want to meet people offline in a relaxed environment such as a bar and talk. And people want to meet in both large groups and small ones, so you need to cater for both types. People will also want personal, one-to-one meetings, both offline and online. I call this kind of meeting a surgery.

The critical success factor for your Club is that you help people, and go on helping them, over and over and over again for hours, days, months and years. It's only by constant, consistent support that you will create a reputation for aiding and assisting people that will stay with you for life.

And people *will* want your help. Some will want advice on which books or magazines to read, or which websites to visit. Others will want introductions and contacts to find jobs, projects or just information. Others will want you to matchmake them with the appropriate person for their skills and talents. This is perhaps the hardest request you'll get. I am asked to matchmake at least five times a day.

There is no limit to what people will ask of you in your role as leader of your Club. But the more you give, the more you will receive. And the greater your reputation will blossom, as the person with the answers.

You might not want to start and lead a Club (although I bet you do). You can always join a Club and contribute rather than lead one. Your membership is of immense value to the members of the groups you join. By participating, you enrich the network around you.

Blogging

Not blagging: blogging. "Blagging" is slang for getting something for nothing, usually with the help of a few lies. "Blogging" also involves free benefits and is, some say, the future (or the downfall) of journalism – so it can't possibly have anything to do with lying, can it?

"Blog", as we have seen, is short for "web log". The original web logs were regularly updated web pages containing links to sites that the creator had found useful, often strung together with commentary. Then some smart people started designing software to help people update their web logs without editing HTML pages.

Blogging software became really popular, because what millions of people want to do on the web is publish their thoughts, their opinions, their gripes, their joys and sometimes the minutiae of their lives for other people to read. They don't want to have to wrestle with HTML code, or maintain a complex site. Bloggers edit their blogs by typing into web forms, and pressing a button when they're finished. The blogging software is typically hosted by a portal site or ISP, though there's nothing to stop you running it on your own server. With the web's premier search engine site Google acquiring blogging leaders Blogger in early 2003, blogging is set to become a permanent feature of the mainstream.

Some have labelled blogging as the net's Next Big Thing. Some bloggers think that they are taking over the role of journalists, and reaching directly to new audiences with new content. Other people – most of them journalists – point out that what the majority of bloggers are writing is opinion, rather than fact. Few blogs break hard news, though some can give national columnists a run for their money.

Ecademy enables blogs for its members. Our blogging software is very easy to use. Our members run blogs on all kinds of subjects. Some use their blogs to clip items of news that catch their notice, and which they want other members to see. Other use them in the traditional way, stitching together links to interesting sites. Some members use their blogs as online diaries, reporting on the development of projects or just keeping friends and browsers up-to-date with their activities. And yet others use their blogs as platforms for sharing their ideas.

Ecademy's blogs add the ability to link comments to individual entries. This means that members can reply to each other's points, add supporting information, or develop a conversation around a theme. Blogging is a very flexible medium, and it seems to support an infinite number of uses.

From the point of view of a networker, blogging has one very important function. Your blog allows you to share knowledge. Remember, giving information away is a key element of networking. Since all Ecademy's blog content is searchable, by posting useful information on your blog, you create new pathways for contacts.

People will read your blog, want to know more about you, click on to your profile, and make contact.

Your blog is therefore contributing to your reputation. By maintaining a blog with good quality entries and useful links, you create a resource that other people will come to rely on. You also signal your own interests and expertise in the best way possible – by demonstrating your involvement. It's easy, and powerful.

Matchmaking

I mentioned that I'm asked to matchmake at least five times every day. Luckily, Ecademy's Member Directory gives me plenty of help.

Members can search in the Directory using personal names, company names or places. It's very easy to locate all the Ecademists in your town, for example. You can email them directly and ask if they'd like to meet up – or ask them to recommend a restaurant, or tell them some juicy gossip about a local celebrity.

You can run sophisticated queries on the directory, combining elements from all the fields that are kept about members. You can, for example, filter your results by industry or occupation.

The Directory can also be sorted. This means that you can view it by name, location, organisation, country and even by "connectedness" – the size of a member's network.

You can also find people in other ways. For example, Ecademy members can enter their fifty words in their personal profile. You can use the "people like this" function to produce a list of people from the directory whose profiles match on their fifty word lists. This would be very time-consuming to do by hand, but the site produces a ranked list of matching members in a matter of moments.

The Member Directory is a fantastic resource. Search it, sort it – play with it. It's full of links that are waiting to be made.

Connecting

Ecademy is all about connecting people. The Member Directory is a great way of connecting, and the platform provides many more. One way of making connections is to see who is currently online. The Ecademy site shows who is currently logged on to the site. If they're registered with an Instant Messaging service, you may be able to start chatting with them right away.

Another way to make connections is to copy messages to people in your network. You won't want to CC everyone you know with every message you send, but keeping relevant contacts in the loop with discussions that might interest them ensures that the network keeps functioning at maximum strength.

The Ecademy platform lets members manage their diaries online too – and to schedule meetings with each other. This is the kind of functionality you might have within your company, if it's a large and enlightened one. We make this kind of intelligent meetings management available across organisational and personal boundaries. You don't have to be running a particular kind of diary software yourself, since all the actions are done through the website.

The platform also lets you make managed introductions to people you don't directly know, but who know someone you wish to meet. It's like having a diary that can reach out to other diaries, and do the initial handshaking for you.

Our site also contains the details of all our offline events. Members can book themselves into these events via the site. They can also generate lists of all the members who have booked for an event. You can even print out a list of attendees, complete with their photographs (if they've supplied them to the Directory). You then have your own, event-specific guidebook to the people who you'll rub shoulders with when you attend. This is a great way of preparing for a successful networking session.

SIGging

Sometimes a Club gets so big it needs the full functionality of the Ecademy platform itself. When this happens – at around 1,000 members – we create a SIG, or Special Interest Group. A SIG is really a cloned version of the full Ecademy site, with its own colour scheme and logos.

People who join an Ecademy SIG become members of Ecademy at the wider level too. But the SIG can display its own member directory, blogs, articles and so on. SIGs tend to be heavy-duty undertakings, and are usually sponsored by corporate members.

Our first SIG was formed to support our members' interest in WiFi technology, and it attracted 1,000 members in just six months. Our second SIG, Beyond Bricks, was launched in April 2003 on behalf of the Department of Trade and Industry. Beyond Bricks is an initiative for internet entrepreneurs founded in 1999.

I expect a thousand SIGs to follow these pioneers. A thousand SIGs, ten thousand clubs, one hundred thousand blogs... There's no limit to how Ecademy can grow to meet the demands of its members. As the technologists say, it'll *scale*.

Informing

Is that enough functionality? The Ecademy platform performs all these functions, and many more. We run a news service called DailEnews that sends headlines, with links to full stories, to members' mailboxes. There are weekly and monthly versions of the news service too.

On the members' content side, as well as the blogging functionality we have a facility for members to upload full articles. These tend to be longer pieces than blog entries, and may act as positioning papers, thought-provokers or reports on industries, trends or projects.

I can't leave the subject of the Ecademy platform without mentioning our Statistics area. We publish *all* our statistics, for everyone to see. You can see the members who have recently joined, and those who visited the site recently. You can check who has contributed the most content to the site – and whose content is most popular with users. You might want to check who the top networkers are, or who's been sending the most invitations to join. (These statistics interest me greatly, because they show me how the network is growing.) And you can see how members rate each other for "reputation", a simple scoring mechanism we use to signal to each other who's been particularly helpful.

The Ecademy platform becomes richer all the time. We're constantly adding new features to it. Come and click around – see what we've got. It's a great place to network.

Climb Aboard

Whatever platform you use to support your networking activities, good tools will help you excel at networking. By taking an organised approach, you can manage the huge volumes of contacts and meetings that you'll need to produce the outcomes you want. Give yourself the tools you need to build and nurture a network that includes 1,000 people for every £100,000 you wish to earn.

You needn't become "a software" yourself, but you'll find yourself increasingly dependent on your tools as your network comes to supply the main needs in your life.

People who network for life rapidly find that their network becomes the source of most of their income, their entertainment and their friendships. They also find that their network naturally absorbs most of their other activities. Networkers become bonded to the platforms that support their activities.

That's why we make every effort to continuously improve the Ecademy platform. We know how important it is to our members. I'd like you to use it and put forward the changes you want to see - just email julian.bond@ecademy.com or glenn.watkins@ecademy.com.

And of course I believe that the Ecademy platform is simply the best place for you to do your networking. It lets you access an awesomely large and varied network of people who are just waiting to connect up with you, and to help you find what you want in life. For all the genius in the technology, it's the people it connects who make the difference.

Chapter 6
The Common Journey

The one with all the names, wins the game

This is the scary chapter. It's the place where I reveal that, whether you like it or not, networking is coming to *your* town, your home, and your heart. It's going to sweep you up and carry you along. And that's good news.

I start by admitting my dark secrets (which, sadly, doesn't take nearly long enough). Then I look at how networking is coming to get you. We learn how Kevin Bacon (or anyone else, for that matter) is only a hop, skip and a jump away, pause to think about social climbing, and plot the history of the future.

The Dark Side

There's a cynical "win friends and influence people" attitude that anyone who claims to be interested in people is doing so only to exploit them. Saying that you love people is a sure way of attracting some odd looks. But I firmly believe that love is the basis of all human health. Love literally keeps us alive. I have three children, which is how I know this to be true.

People sometimes say to me: Your take on networking all seems very open and transparent and sensible and natural – where's the catch? Where's *the dark bit*?

It's hard for people to accept that anyone who wants to lead on the habits and principles of networking doesn't have something to hide.

The only dark secret I have is that I support Chelsea.

I don't have the time, and I don't have the cast of mind, to develop a dark secret. I don't have any agenda other than building a fabulous network. That's all there is. It's not much: it's just everything.

Everyone Needs to Network

You might be thinking by now, I need to go out and network. That's true enough, except that networking is coming to find you – ready or not. You're caught up in the logic of networking, whether you're seeking involvement or whether you'd prefer to hide. It comes back to the maths.

Here's how the new maths of networking affects you.

Your network needs to contain 1,000 people for every £100,000 you want to earn. If you don't have a network, you won't be putting bread on your table. This is the economic reality of our young century. Get used to it. Your children will be taught networking skills at school – it's networking that will ensure their economic futures. You're just going to have to school yourself. That's what I've done.

You know that there's no such thing as a job for life any more, if there ever was. And what a relief it is to know that all of us will enjoy variety, and self-determination, and continued learning, during our lives. That we won't be expected to sign up to life on a corporate ladder, with a gold watch at the end for good behaviour. We're responsible for building our own lives, and for deciding the levels of luxury and risk we apply to our lives. It's exhilarating – and maybe frightening.

The good news is that networkers are not born, they are made. They are not Lucky Fools, but smart, active pursuers of encounters. They are taught and trained. Anyone can be a networker, and everyone must be a networker.

People sometimes say to me: Networking isn't me. It's just not me.

And I agree with them. Because until you network, networking *isn't* you. How could it be? At one time, you couldn't read. Luckily, you probably weren't given the option of saying: Reading isn't me. It was something you had to learn. You learned, and you changed. You can learn to network. And you must learn to network. And you will learn to network – *by* networking.

Networking will make you rich, and rich in more than money.

Back to school

There was once a time when nobody learned Marketing as a subject. That's hard to believe now, when Marketing is entrenched as a core business discipline and expands into new territories every day.

People will one day marvel that Networking was not seen as a subject worthy of study, research and practical application.

I believe that we will soon see a prestigious and active Institute of Networking. Its conferences will be awesome. The Institute will have to book venues where the corridors and cafés take up more combined floor space than the presentation halls!

By 2020 at the latest, we will be able to study for a BA in Networking, and even an MN: a Master of Networking. These courses will, of course, be highly networked, with student exchanges a core part of the curriculum. And there will even be Doctors of Networking: gurus of human connectivity, researching into the invisible forces that bring us together and transmit energy amongst us.

Meanwhile schools and universities will be rated for their "quality of network" and ranked accordingly in league tables. Each institution's value will therefore be partly based on how well it helps its people generate and sustain connections – recognising the crucial role of networking in the economy.

Everybody Connected

Most people assume that celebrities are surrounded by warmth and interest. The reverse is usually the case. Celebrities – our new gods – are isolated by our adulation. If they try to lead regular lives they are pursued by the long lens of the media.

Anyone, at any "top", is likely to be professionally lonely. Did you know that you can reach out to people at "the top"? That you can discover their "nodeness" in a random connection?

You may have heard of the "six degrees of separation" theory. This theory states that we are *all* connected to each other through, at most, six intermediary steps. As the old song had it, I've danced with a girl who's danced with a man who's danced with a girl who's danced with the Prince of Wales...

Famously, some smart folks have worked out that you can always get to actor Kevin Bacon through six or fewer other actors that he's appeared with in movies. In other words, if you want to reach Kevin Bacon, you can start with pretty much any Hollywood name. (But be polite: Bacon is probably getting a little tired of this game by now. There's a safe way of doing it at the definitive "Six Degrees of Kevin Bacon" website at http://www-distance.syr.edu/bacon.html.)

In Ecademy we have implemented a "friend of a friend" function that takes advantage of networked connectedness. A user of Ecademy can ask the software to plot a route to any individual within the network, starting with people that you know. You can then use each connection in the route to make an introductory step, so building your way to the goal piece by piece.

Does that sound scary? It's a very powerful feature, and the first time you use it, it *is* scary. That's because the feature speeds up something we're familiar with in everyday life, *and* makes it available on demand when we're used to it being rarely available.

Here's what I mean by speeding up. In the offline networking world, you might ask a neighbour if he knows anyone who's had a kitchen installed recently and could recommend a good fitter. He thinks Marie at his office might be happy with her new kitchen (she keeps talking about it!), and he'll ask her to give you a call when he next sees her. This process is slow, and it's flaky. It might work, it might not.

Making the same appeal in an online community can make connections across networks in real time. Some Ecademy connections occur this way, through instant messaging. Many Ecademy connections occur in the near-real time of email.

And here's what I mean about the rare availability of "friend of a friend" features in the offline world. Our ordinary, everyday world isn't being recorded or stored anywhere. The relationships which underpin it are kept alive by our enacting them. There's no "brain" that can map a route through our social networks. When we use the "friend of a friend" approach in ordinary life, it's like casting a message in a bottle into the waves. It's very rarely that we find ourselves in a situation where we can use "friend of a friend" with confidence.

The "old boy networks" or elites of the past created selective networks that guaranteed the availability of "friend of a friend" functionality. The old school tie acted as a visible sign of members' connectedness. These networks erected high barriers to entry and defended them doggedly.

Over time, these elite networks have degraded. Their influence has reduced in a world that grows ever more meritocratic.

But the functions they performed, in their limited way, were very powerful for their members. Some people say that the old elites have retained their power, but learned to hide it better. There might be some truth in this, but it's hard to measure.

Modern technology allows us to build and join networks that surpass the reach of traditional human networks, and which telescope the time needed to generate benefits from networking. These new networks are much more inclusive, flexible and robust. They're also transparent. Outsiders can see what they are for, and what they are doing. They can also join without passing discriminatory tests.

The name Ecademy honours the networks of the past. The original "academy" was Plato's garden near Athens. The online dimension of Ecademy creates an unimaginably large garden which anyone can enter, and where anyone can discuss life or business (or even philosophy) with anyone else. Ecademy's offline dimension lets us anchor the garden in real cities, real membership groups and real lives.

"Academy" went on to mean any place where people studied. But it quickly acquired a sense of exclusivity. The E of Ecademy means "everyone". Our school tie is available to all.

The Climbing Club

There's a set of would-be networkers who are distinct from the January Joggers we met earlier, and rather more worrisome to committed networkers like myself. January Joggers may convert to lifetime members of the networking community. Social climbers, on the other hand, usually lose their hold.

Let's be clear. Networking isn't a polite name for advancing yourself socially. Networking does "open doors", but they're not necessarily doors in a social hierarchy. If you see the world in terms of a pyramid, then networking will disappoint you. You'll also be a disappointment to the network – some members of which will be genuinely in a position to help you.

I've noticed that some high-profile networkers regard networking as a means of accessing the best restaurants, the best-known decision-makers and the best-bred families. Well, I *do* find that networking leads me to the best of everything the world has to offer. The difference is, I don't start out with a set idea of what "the best" is. I don't buy anyone's rich list. I'm seeking other riches.

If you really just want to climb a hierarchy that someone else has defined, then it isn't networking you want but entryism. You need to worm your way into the traditional clubs and associations, the closed ranks of the elite.

You need to take on their beliefs and ape their attitudes. You need to abandon the modern world and live in the past. And maybe you'll make it. But I have to warn you: that old world is shrinking every day. It's growing ever more irrelevant. Its power is fading. Do you really want to reach another "top" – only to find it's not the top of anything any more?

Think about where we look for authority in today's world. At the domestic purchasing level, we prefer recommendations from our friends to cold sales made to us on the phone. When it comes to making choices for our families, we look to other families for guidance.

We might look at league tables when we're choosing a school, for example, but in the end we're going to pick the place that *feels* right for our child; and that feeling is going to come from the teachers and parents and children who are already in the school. Schools express themselves in this very personal and direct way because they are networks too.

In matters of politics, we tend not to trust our representatives. We're cynical about the motives of politicians, confused by their party groupings and bored with voting. But we campaign passionately for the issues in which we believe, and we express our approval and protest through the products and messages we choose to consume. We're no longer sitting, waiting to be told what to think. We refer to each other for guidance on how we should be shaping the world around us.

The traditional seats of power represent strategies for success in a different world: the past. Their energy has leaked away, but it has not evaporated. It's all around us, permeating our society. It sparks to life when we connect with each other. It breathes in our conversations. It lights up rooms, and lights up lives.

We're used to the idea that success is about climbing. But networking shows us that happiness – in business, and in life – is about reaching out to people in *all* directions. We may stand on the shoulders of giants, in that we're privileged by the discoveries and sacrifices of previous generations, but we don't need to trample each other in some mad scramble to the top of a heap. We've got to let all those images go. They're spreading isolation and conflict.

I hope you'll embrace networking as a way of growing, and as a way of being part of something that is also growing. I believe networking means the same thing as joining the human race. And that's not a race that anyone can win.

The Journey Ahead

Where is Ecademy in its journey?

1998 was our year of founding. You know what the foundation period is like: late nights, scribbled-on beer mats and crossed fingers.

1999 was the year we launched. We spent our time communicating the Ecademy message one-on-one to key influencers, and enrolling them as members. In January 1999 we had our first 27 members.

Fiona Blows was member number 10 and remains with us. David Alschuler from the Aberdeen Group was member 22. Andy Matson from Microsoft was member 25. All remain on board and gunning for our cause.

In 2000 we boomed. Interest in everything online was driving members to join in unprecedented numbers.

But in 2001 we experienced our recession. The hype escaped from the dotcom bubble, and our membership declined.

2002 was our year of pain. We had to decide how we were going to reposition Ecademy, make it relevant to people's lives, and grow in utility and influence. We built our first long-term supplier relationship when Julian Bond morphed our website into a fledgling networking platform, complete with automated membership features.

2003 opened with 13,760 confirmed members, compared to 2002's opening of 10,500. This is the year of rebirth. We emerged from pain into light. Why are we experiencing growth, when the economy remains in the doldrums and bitterness over the dotcom hype lingers? It may be because our software platform is exceptional. It may be because our offline events are so popular. Perhaps it's the subscription services we began introducing at the tail end of 2002. Or perhaps we're just being swept along in the fashion for networking.

I see 2004 as the year of excitement. We'll be consolidating our growth, extending our services and proving that Ecademy is no fashion victim.

2005 will be the year of thrill, as the excitement becomes visible. Success stories born of Ecademy connections will start to gain traction in the media.

I predict 2006 will be the year of – rock and roll! The market for IPOs will return with a vengeance as technology and business process innovations hit the mainstream. 2006 will make 1996's peak year for IPOs look tame. Ecademy will be in the thick of the action.

In 2007 we'll be going global. Fully functioning Ecademy cells will be active in major cities. Local differences will add to Ecademy strengths to produce potent networking solutions for far-flung markets.

And in 2008 there will be fledgling Ecademy cells in 1,000 cities worldwide. You'll be able to find an Ecademist friend wherever you travel. The online and offline dimensions of Ecademy will be united across the globe.

By 2050, we aim to have ten million members, or 10,000 members in each of 1,000 cities. Ecademy's founders will be 86 years old!

You'll notice that I view our history and future in terms of human emotions: pain, excitement and so on. That's because whatever I'm doing with Ecademy, I never forget that it's about people. And that it's *only* about people.

The only numbers I have to show you are membership numbers – because, as we've seen, networking is partly about volume of connections. I don't show earnings graphs, because I regard Ecademy not as an economic vehicle, but an economic *engine*. It's a cause, a movement. It's my life. It's your life too.

Into the Light

I believe that while networking as a phenomenon has always been present in our culture, it is now assuming the role of the economy's main engine. I present the history and future of Ecademy's development because it demonstrates how our networking organisation simultaneously rides and feeds the emergence of networking as the key factor of market success. It's through networks that the new companies and industries of the future will be created. Networks will provide the paths to delivery for novel discoveries and processes. And networks will bind us together in a climate of richness, and potential, and hope.

Reject the idea that networking is a simple technique for the self-interested. Forget the idea that networking is about exclusive clubs, or flattery, or deceit, or any of the other unsavoury practices that are sometimes identified with it. Networking does not have a dark side. It is, in a very simple sense, the practice of openness.

When we network, we make ourselves open to people and to ideas. We suspend our interest in predefined outcomes. We come out to play. We are ourselves.

If you want a harsh message – one that will force you out into the network as an active member – then look no further than the highly connected nature of the world around you. Can you afford to be outside the network?

I'd go further than this. Not only can you not afford to be outside the network: *the network will not let you remain outside.* The jobs, the institutions, the professions, the activities that remain unaffected by networking are becoming ever more scarce.

For example, you might find a job from a "help wanted" ad, but you know that advertised jobs are the tip of the jobs iceberg. And you also know that *all* the opportunities defined and packaged as "jobs" are just the tip of an even greater iceberg: all the roles that need filling and tasks that need doing, if only the people with the needs could bump into the people with the skills. A "job" is a kind of connection between a need and a solution. Networking *is* connecting. Networking makes visible, and solves, huge numbers of such needs – numbers that make the formal "job market" look tiny.

I predict that on current trends *all* jobs will be performed by self-employed contractors by 2030. There will then be one stark fact: if you don't network, you don't eat!

Of course, there won't just be a "big bang" when the economy switches over from traditional employment to self-employment.

It is happening gradually, little by little, day by day –
although the media sector transitioned to networks of
independent contractors in a handful of years.
Choosing to ignore networking is therefore a very
risky strategy. And since networks take time to build,
the time to start building is now.

I hope you're starting to see that networking *is* you.
It's your passport to the future, your invitation to the
party. Don't pass it up.

Chapter 7
Speeding Up Serendipity

The weak links are the strongest

Warning: this chapter contains philosophy. If you're in any way allergic to thinking about the fundamentals of how we all survive and thrive on this planet, then you need to skip this chapter. Go for a nap, and we'll pick you up later.

How deep does the philosophy get? Only as deep as the nearest river, which I'm going to ask you to stand in. Only as deep as the concept of happiness, and its relationship to randomness.

And after the deep stuff, we surface in the midst of modern corporate life. I ask why corporations are bad at networking, and suggest how they can improve their performance.

I ask you to recognise – and abandon – your comfort zone. It's the only way that you'll expand your networking horizons.

Finally, we return to the river, but this time in the company of three legendary princes who taught how randomness brings riches – long before the word "networking" was born.

Enriched Relationships

The philosopher Heraclitus saw the world as being in a state of constant change, or flux. He memorably said that "it is not possible to stand in the same river twice".

I was reminded of this saying when I heard about a virgin entrepreneur who found the launch funding for a new business – while standing in a river. He was (you guessed it) on a fishing trip with an old friend. They got to talking about current projects, and the entrepreneur mentioned the new company, and the funds they were seeking. His friend listened, cast his hook, and offered the money.

The two fishermen had a long relationship, but they had never been in business together. As they stood together in that river – a river they could never stand in again – one of the friends took the decision to risk changing the nature of their relationship. He didn't ask for money. He merely answered his friend's question.

He had not cultivated this friendship so that one day it would pay a dividend. He had not pursued his friend as a prospective frog-prince.

But equally, he did not shy away from the opportunity to reach out to his friend when it arose.

Did our budding entrepreneur break the rules of friendship? Did he pollute the river of life?

I think that, in that moment in that river, our two friends decided to change the scope of their relationship. They opted to add a new dimension to their shared life. In doing so, they both grew.

We are all standing in a river, if only we knew it.

One Ecademist tells me that he first met a valued business partner when they were exercising their dogs together in the park. When two people love the same breed of dog, it's likely they will share other tastes and values too. They will have a good opening reason to trust each other's judgement. That's not a bad start to a relationship. It's random, but it's meaningful.

Some relationships decay through lack of attention. Others change out of all recognition as the parties adjust the relationship to take into account changes in their own situations and goals. Some evaporate when the heat is turned up too high. But few react poorly to enrichment.

Network Karma

The lesson I take from these stories, and from the countless other instances of network serendipity that I experience personally and hear about from other Ecademists, is that our ability to reach out to each other enriches our environment. Humans thrive on communication and interaction. It's almost as if our actions create a kind of nourishment. By connecting with each other, we generate fuel.

Some people believe that the deeds we do are somehow absorbed by the universe and turned into good (or bad) fortune. They believe, at a very deep level, in the interconnectedness of all life. These beliefs have long and respectable heritages in some of the world's major religions, especially those of the east.

You don't have to be a mystic to notice that the way we behave has a direct impact on the immediate world around us.

You don't need to imagine waves of cause and effect rippling through the fabric of the universe to appreciate that when someone cuts you up in traffic, it can make you scowl at the next person you see. You know that the sincerity with which you treat people calibrates their response to you: your openness will activate their openness.

Now add the effects of network arithmetic to these simple, localised situations and that networked, responsive universe starts to emerge – of its own accord. I know it's hard to believe that a smile can really infect the entire world. But then, think about this: Where do jokes come from? Some of them are written by professionals, it's true. But most of them just appear, and are passed on. They spread virally. They have lives of their own.

There's been lots of academic and mainstream discussion around Richard Dawkins's concept of the *meme*. A meme is the cultural equivalent of a gene.

It's a unit of meaning that replicates itself within populations of hosts. Jokes, opinions, catchphrases, policies, tastes – these are all types of meme.

I think something analogous to the meme operates in the dimension of networking. When we reach out to each other, some invisible unit of value is created and transferred. I have no idea what this unit is, or what we should call it. But I know that many other people sense its existence as well. It's the elusive fundamental particle of the networked universe.

The network thinker Cory Doctorow calls the stuff Whuffie. In his novel *Down and Out in the Magic Kingdom*, Whuffie is a mixture of currency and karma. People are awarded Whuffie based on how helpful their acts are.

They use Whuffie to transact goods and services. It's a system that only makes sense in a networked world, and – importantly – a world where people see their interrelationships as the drivers of wealth, respect and happiness. Incidentally, although Doctorow's book is available through traditional channels, he has also made it freely available for download (see http://www.craphound.com/down/).

The Ecademy platform includes a rating system that members can use to show their appreciation of others. The system doesn't extend to individual interactions between members, although there's nothing to stop us implementing such a feature if our members demand it. But whether you can put a name to this karmic currency, and whether you account for it strictly, don't really matter.

It's more important that you can *imagine* your acts having a value in the community. Your ability to envision the value of your acts will invest them with greater power.

Happiness is Luckiness

Look up the word *happy* in the dictionary and you'll see that the first definition given is "lucky". Our word *happy* comes from the old word *hap*, meaning luck. *Happen* shares the same root. What happens is luck, and luck makes us happy.

The randomness, or hap-iness, of events can bring us happiness.

Think for a moment of the US Constitution, and its commitment to "the pursuit of happiness". More than two hundred years after it was created, this phrase is still compelling. It means not only that people have a right to be happy, but that they can *pursue* happiness.

The entrepreneurial spirit of the United States is based on the notion that you can make your own luck. I think this is true, in the sense that you can generate randomness in your life.

Let's bring these ideas down to the day-to-day level of business. How do randomness and happiness stack up as strategies in the face of targeting and... misery? Think of selling. The heartbreaking part of selling is making cold calls. Nobody likes making cold calls. Many people make cold calls for a living, and many of them do it superbly well.

But ask them if they'd rather use a different means of reaching potential customers, and they will bite your arm off. It's just not natural to prefer the cold to the warmth.

What is a cold call? It's an intrusion by one stranger in the life of another. The first stranger has something definite to sell. The second stranger has been selected because she lives in a particular postcode, or because she once bought a particular product, or on some other pretext. The call is founded on the caller's proposition that a transaction should take place.

Contrast that with networking. Networking is not about intruding on strangers, but on collecting friends. A networking encounter is never a cover for a sales pitch. Networkers range widely in their conversations, and they listen to each other. They don't have fixed agendas. They enjoy the ride. Ninety-eight times out of one hundred, nothing tangible occurs as a direct result of the encounter.

And, over the distance, networking produces better results than cold calling.

Ecademy is blazing a new business trail. We're banishing the cold call to the past. The fear and distaste that go along with cold calling are being banished too. The depressing logic of cold calling – that every call should produce a sale, so most calls are failures – is being replaced by the more heartening facts of the new network maths. And the notion of a sales world that is essentially confrontational is being torn down to make way for a more relaxed, more expansive, more diverse, more human, more creative and more fun way of doing business.

I think we're lucky to be living in the age we find ourselves in. The old business models don't work any more. Technology has not removed the need for people to interact with each other – quite the reverse. We're exposed to a world of unlimited possibilities. We make our own luck, our own hap-iness. And we make it together.

Helping Corporations Network

Networking is replacing traditional forms of doing business. It is flooding in to occupy the space abandoned by mass marketing. You would therefore think that corporations were getting a handle on networking, and investing in developing their networking skills. Sadly, few of them are.

Why are corporations slow to embrace networking?

Some of the reasons are structural. You'll notice that the investment banks have Mergers and Acquisitions teams, but not Getting-To-Know-Each-Other teams. Business is structured around ownership of entities, rather than around partnerships in value creation. As the business establishment begins to measure and account for network effects better, you'll see the traditional service players begin to offer advice on networking.

But that's some way off. Today, none of the traditional advisors is leaning heavily on its corporate clients and spelling out the realities of the networked world.

Other structural reasons relate to the way corporations regard themselves. They tend to see themselves as self-contained. They express this self-sufficiency in their physical locations. It's not just the gleaming glass and granite towers that some corporations use to demonstrate their solidity, aspirations and status. It's also the fact that they *imprison* their people within those buildings.

Companies erect firewalls around their organisations – technical ones and cultural ones. On the technology front, it makes sense to isolate your network from viruses and other nasty bugs that bring your systems down or violate the privacy of your data. But in the cultural realm – the realm of ideas, innovation and growth – germs are a good thing. Germs of new ideas and new practices, or memes, or whatever you want to call them, are the raw material of change. If corporates do not expose themselves to regular infection from outside, they die.

The fact is, most people who work for corporations aren't allowed out to play during the day. And many of them are too tired to network in the evenings. Add to that the message they're given about the company's self-sufficiency, and there's little motivation to network in today's large companies.

If you're a large, successful company that has been operating for generations, has units around the world and has even invented much of the technology and methodology of your industry, then you're likely to believe that the source of every solution can be found within the company.

The company is, after all, a historically proven way of efficiently gathering and deploying resources.

At the same time, the all-purpose, all-caring paternalistic corporation of the past has given way to the leaner, downsized and rightsized corporation that uses outsourcing and flexible employee relationships to its benefit. Many large companies have hollowed out their infrastructure and their employee benefits while trying to maintain the impression of being powerful yet caring organisations. They've given up self-sufficiency, but not encouraged their people to look elsewhere for the resources and opportunities they need. And when their attentions do turn to the value of their people, companies often latch on to the loathsome idea that human being are "assets" to be "sweated".

Another reason why corporations rarely "get" networking is that they quickly become distracted by the related technologies. This is understandable, and it's the responsibility of all of us networkers to explain that networking is about people, not machines. I'm under no illusions that technology underpins serious networking activities, or I wouldn't have invested so heavily in the Ecademy platform. But the platform only makes sense in the context of networking as a human activity that humans value. I can't – and I won't – persuade some company to invest in a networking platform just because I think such things are cool (although I do think they're cool). But I will – and I do – evangelise on behalf of networking within companies whenever I get the opportunity.

I'll push the systems to one side and focus on the fundamentals: network maths, randomness, volume – all the topics we're examining in this book.

I've seen some "lite" forms of networking applied in corporations, under various different names but with uniformly poor results. These initiatives tend to be presented as communications exercises, whereby people from different parts of the business get to meet each other and appreciate each other's roles. This is great, as far as it goes – but it doesn't go very far. True networks can't be circumscribed. They grow according to their own dynamics. They take root in unpredictable ways. And they produce unexpected outcomes.

The irony is that most successful corporations are successful *because of* their unacknowledged, inbuilt networks. Companies like 3M or IBM produce innovations because their research and development staffs are allowed to follow their own research priorities, are encouraged to interfere with each other's projects, and are allowed to mix in the wider research communities at universities. Most of us can cite experiences from corporate life where a great product or service was developed, or an impressive saving was made, because certain people got talking to each other across organisational boundaries. We know that the production of great ideas goes up when teams go offsite for training or team-building – and that the rate skyrockets in the bar and at the dinner table when the formal agenda is over.

I'd go so far as to say that today's leading companies owe their success to the cultivation of connectedness and randomness. This isn't chaos, because connectedness *creates* structure. But I understand why few corporations advertise the immense contribution of network effects to their business. It makes the traditional role of management sound, well, redundant.

And that's where we'll find the key to igniting networking within corporations as a conscious force, rather than an unacknowledged one. We need business leaders to act as networking role models. We need business leaders to increase their volume of encounters. We need them to put the management cycle of goal-measure-goal-measure to one side and address a higher responsibility. We need them to demonstrate to all their people that it's okay – more than okay – to get out of the building and make new contacts. That the sales and marketing departments don't have the monopoly on communications. That killer ideas aren't going to be bought in from some catalogue. And that reaching out to people is the fundamental step in the new dance of business.

Beyond the Comfort Zone

If you stay in the same group of people, then your network won't expand. If you inhabit the same mental framework, your mind will decay. You need to challenge yourself with new ideas if you're going to keep growing as a person. And you need to expand your activities into new areas if you're to make new links.

I would guess that the average person knows about two hundred people. Half of these are friends, and half derive from business activities. Of course I hope that the two categories overlap, so that your business associates are also friends, and so that you would consider buying from your friends too.

I know many directors of leading global companies who meet four people every day, five days a week. It's clear at the top of our top businesses that networking is a vital function.

But as we know, in a fully functioning networked world, everybody is a "top". We all need to acquire the behaviour of the best networkers.

Now, the average business person might meet as many as one hundred people in a year. That's clearly not going to be enough to produce any useful network effects. So, to increase your network, you need to pursue its growth actively.

One way to do this is to make friends within *walks of life*.

Walking the walks of life
Aim to have friends in every –

- City
- Region
- Country
- Industry
- Science

- Art
- Sport
- Faith

And aim to expand this list of categories every day.

The Three Princes

There is a series of Persian fairy tales in which three princes, who live on a distant island, make new discoveries by combining their wisdom with accidental events.

In one of the stories the princes meet, by a river, a merchant who is crying with grief and cursing the gods. He tells the princes that he had built a palace to house all the treasures he had acquired on his travels. But the river has overflowed its banks, and swept all his wealth away. The princes confuse the merchant by congratulating him on his great blessing, and they ride away.

Several years later, they happen to return to the river. A servant greets them, and invites them to the palace of his master, which sits high above the river. There they meet and dine with the merchant, who tells them how, after the princes left, he sat by the river and listened to its sound, just as he had done when he was a boy. And how the river told him to look up, and see a better place.

He quickly realised that by building his palace on the higher ground, he would have a better view of the river.

But as he began to clear the ground for his new palace, he discovered that the site was a field of fabulous gems. This new-found wealth, to which he had been led by the river, enabled him to build a magnificent new palace.

And the merchant did not keep his good fortune to himself:

I invited all that I knew from all the kingdoms that I travelled through, to partake of my hospitality. And those weary trailers that I did not know I bid them to rest and refresh themselves.

Everyone came and each brought me treasures to fill my many rooms, but the greatest of treasures is their company and friendship for that is more precious than all the wealth in the kingdoms.[2]

These three princes, who gloried in the randomness of life, lived on the island of Serendip, which we now know as Sri Lanka. In 1754, Horace Walpole coined the word *serendipity* to mean the art of "making discoveries, by accidents and sagacity", in the mode of the three princes. He also noted that the princes discovered "things which they were not in quest of".

Walpole's word has survived in our language, though the tales of the princes are scattered and little known.

---

[2]

http://www.angelfire.com/emo/serendipityato/three_princes_of_se rendip.htm

These princes are different from the heroes of European stories, who were indeed engaged in "quests". The Princes of Serendip embody the principles that I've been exploring in this book. They are, above all, open to randomness. They expect nothing from their encounters, yet they experience great riches. And the lives that they touch are illuminated with the simple wisdom that real wealth is to be found in "company and friendship".

These three princes are my heroes. They have the courage to roam, to engage, and to celebrate the creative randomness of life. They teach us that the river of life is to be experienced, to be venerated – and to be listened to.

Random connections generate more wealth than targeted ones. Ecademy's primary purpose in the networked economy is to manufacture randomness. Say goodbye to the smoke-and-mirrors companies of the dotcom bubble and get to recognise the new industries on the skyline. We use raw social energy to forge connections. The structures we build are strong, flexible and robust. They travel across markets and geographies. They serve in the foundations of strong, healthy businesses.

Members of Ecademy benefit from the organisation's randomness in terms of links: and the money's in the links not the nodes. If you're not an active member of a broad networking organisation like Ecademy, you may suffer from a scarcity of randomness.

Another way of putting all this is to say that we're speeding up serendipity. We're providing the Princes of Serendip with motorised transport. We're helping them get around their island more quickly, so they can make more discoveries, and infect more people with their marvellous appetite for life. And we're also helping our princes to grow their island, so that it overlaps the world exactly.

Chapter 8
In The Event

Your face is your brand

So much for maths, and technology, and philosophy.
What's it like to network in the flesh? (Don't worry:
you get to keep your clothes on.)

This chapter includes tips for getting the most out of
networking events, dealing with times of scarcity and
abundance, and working around shyness.

Goals at Networking Events

In my experience, people who attend networking
events are seeking one or more of just three things:

- Knowledge

- Contacts

- Transactions

That's fine; but networkers should also be looking for
these things:

- Fun

- Laughter

- Joy
- Hope
- Love

See what I mean? We're talking about networking for life – so add life to your networking.

Let's look again at those top three goals. Firstly, knowledge.

Gathering knowledge is a low-profile activity and it's hard to upset anybody by doing it. We all love to talk about ourselves, and to share our knowledge. Networking events are indeed great learning environments.

I don't buy the notion that networking events are the only place you can acquire knowledge. Consider a trade show in your industry. You may go there to learn about partners and competitors in your industry. But the most important things you learn won't come from the company literature you might pick up. Nor will your key learnings come from the company pitches you hear. Let's face it, you could pick all that stuff up from the website, without leaving the comfort of your chair.

But you will learn plenty at the trade show. You'll be able to measure the location and strength of the buzz around different companies and products. You'll be able to talk with other visitors, as well as the folks on the stands. And you'll be able to ask the exhibitors direct questions that cut through their standard texts.

(Believe me, they *want* you to challenge them. It helps get the blood out of their tired feet and into their brains.)

So, you can certainly use networking events to gather knowledge. But don't use them to trawl for information that you could get elsewhere. You should be gathering information constantly in your daily activities, not waiting for a social opportunity to take it in passively.

You should also be prepared to give your knowledge. Just to make that plain, perhaps I should say that you must be prepared to *give away* your knowledge. At every opportunity. Why should anyone share important information with you if you're not prepared to do the same? And I don't mean that you should be able to swap information of equal value with anyone who has information that might aid you. These are not one-for-one swaps. I mean that you should attend networking events with the attitude of an information-giver. Recognise that knowledge shared is knowledge squared. Delight in the power of conversation to bring context and unexpected utility to facts. Abandon any sense that most of your knowledge is private or too valuable to give away: keep it to yourself, and you might as well not have it. Focus on the Give and Take Ratio: the successful networker's life is 98% Give and 2% Take.

Your knowledge needs to be shown the light, or it will die. It won't do you any good if it's locked up in your head. Your knowledge needs to be set free so that it can be used by other people to create new opportunities and new ideas. It needs freedom to seek out and merge with other knowledge.

You need to give your knowledge a life of its own, so that it can work for you and for the network.

Now let's look at the second goal: contacts. Networking events are clearly, on one level, about acquiring contacts. That's how it should be.

You know you need volume and variety in your network, so go for it. But you should also *bring* contacts to the event. There are two senses to this. You can physically bring people to the event, and introduce them. This is perhaps the highest service we can do for someone in our network. The other way you can bring your contacts to the event is to share your contact database.

And don't be content with making one or two introductions at the one event. Look for volume here too. Be a mixer – be a connector. Aim to connect up people that you meet *during* the event. Put people together, and let them develop their relationship. See how many great, enduring and enriching connections you can catalyse with a few seconds of introductory work spread throughout a gathering. You can create sparks, and watch the energy you release flow through a room, liberating people and – who knows – possibly changing the paths of their lives forever.

Notice that our needs for knowledge and contacts are *open*. We cannot have enough of either. And we can share our knowledge and contacts without using them up.

But the third goal that people seek from networking events is closed. Transactions, or deals, form the basic atomic level of business. As I've suggested throughout this book, if you come to networking with the expectation of being offered deals, you will be frustrated. Conversely, if you bring a sack full of money to a networking event you will be welcomed with open arms (but probably by the wrong people).

You should therefore forget about transactions when you're at a networking event. If a transaction becomes a possibility during a conversation, you'll know all about it. If it doesn't, then that just fits the maths.

Your main conscious activity, then, is going to be *sharing* knowledge and contacts. And the best thing about this is that you can, at a pinch, do it without any preparation. Assuming you're gathering information and contacts as part of your daily activities, then you're already beautifully prepared for any networking event. Because when you do so, you're always networking. Your life has become a networking event – and the odd moment when it's enlivened by chardonnay and name badges is simply one of the smoothest patches. Once you realise that you have become a habitual networker, you will also recognise that the sharing of knowledge and contacts is a kind of transaction too – perhaps the most valuable kind.

Dedicated networkers will want to add two ingredients to this recipe for success. The first is an emotional, or spiritual, ingredient. As well as concentrating on sharing, dedicated networkers focus on lifting the spirits of those with whom they interact.

They strive to make genuine, personal contact with people. They open themselves to the possibilities of life-changing friendships. They relish the opportunity to see the world anew, through a new friend's eyes.

The second ingredient is preparation. Although you can get by with no preparation, and enjoy a relaxed and successful networking event, you'll get more out of it if you do a little homework beforehand. Check out the people who are registered to attend. Remember, if it's an Ecademy event you can print out the attendee list together with their photos. You can also check out attendees' fifty word profiles, in order to key into people's interests and predict some useful conversation topics.

You can also add some pre-emptive structure to the event by booking appointments ahead of time. Many people appreciate appointments being made, even though the broad format of a networking event is fluid. This is partly because pre-arranged appointments make for points of certainty amidst the fluidity. They also give your contacts an opportunity to do their preparation on you. And they act as an incentive for both parties to attend.

Dealing with Nothing

Given the stark maths of networking, and the fact that its returns, though substantial, come in random bursts, it's inevitable that much of the networking experience is filled with apparently pointless detail. Networking generates lots of activity, and lots of information.

It also generates transactions, but these tend to pop up in distant parts of the machine, and they are usually separated in time from the interactions that give them their birth. How do you keep the faith when the rewards seem so rare, distant and uncontrollable?

The key to dealing with this inescapable aspect of networking is to let go of your urge to control the overall process. You can't shape what the network will deliver. It is not a machine that can be programmed, but an organism that is nurtured by masses of separate, yet interlinked, contributing nodes. You might as well try to control the weather.

It would be great to suggest that we can all find some zen-like lack of concern about the outcomes of our investments. I know some people who can indeed achieve this state of detachment. My only observation here is that having a fortune helps.

And the kind of fortune I mean is the luck of a loving family and a commitment to networking for its human value.

For those of us who can't maintain an icy calm during periods of drought I suggest that we take care to exert control over the things we *can* control. Like volume. Volume carried me though 2001 to 2003, the most difficult times in the economy in my twenty year career. When nothing seems to be coming from my network, I'm spurred to enlarge my network, and to refresh my existing contacts. I look for new walks of life to explore, new ideas to feed on. I get together with people and talk what-if's, and football.

And I keep my mind trained on the fact that networking is a continuous investment, and a form of insurance. I control the things I can control, and I let the universe take care of itself. I don't shake my fist at the rain, because I've got an umbrella.

Overwhelmed by Abundance

Networkers know that while periods of drought are spooky, they're nothing compared to the times when your network over-delivers. And it will. You'll be sowing so many seeds, opening up so many potential avenues, that at times you'll have too many opportunities arriving at the same time.

The reaction of most people to an abundance of opportunities presented by their network is one of pride, swiftly overtaken by panic. How am I going to do all those projects? Who should I let down? How should I go about disappointing them?

This reaction is honest and understandable. But it's all wrong. It's wrong in every possible sense.

In the first place, I doubt that we should feel pride when the network delivers. It makes more sense to feel proud of the millions of small inputs that we make to the input, since it is these that ultimately deliver. In the second place, the networker's answer to over-demand is not to close down the number of options to a comfortable, personal level. The networker *uses the network* to deal with abundance.

Too many great projects being suggested to you? Well, who is there in your network who could take some of them on?

Could you work with some colleagues to share the opportunities? Or could you refer the work on to them, and step aside entirely? You won't be doing the network, or yourself, any favours if you accept too many opportunities and then fail to deliver on them. That will only tend to corrode your status as a node. But sharing your harvest will create additional value in the network. Sharing will ensure the jobs get done, strengthen existing links in the network, and create new ones. The network's random abundance can be fed back into the network to amplify its power to the benefit of all its members. And your reputation will soar.

Working Round Shyness

Shyness isn't a rare condition. It strikes even the most outgoing people from time to time. We're wrong when we say that there are "shy people". To use "shy" as a label puts people into a box. If you call yourself "shy", you give yourself a label to live up to. Even if you are shy in many social situations, there will be many more occasions when you're not. The difference often comes down to getting round the initial contact. That's the part that we fear.

I believe that people's fear in new social situations comes down to the mistaken belief that they have to *perform* in some way.

That they have to pretend to be something they're not. Along with this supposed need to pretend, there's the idea that we must present a favourable image of ourselves. This notion, in turn, sparks anxiety that the people we meet want something from us – something that we can't predict, and probably can't supply.

All this frantic imagining goes on day after day, in a billion heads across the planet. At the same time, people get on with the business of meeting, connecting and conversing. We shove these anxieties apart. We challenge them. Or we accept them, and get on with networking anyway.

I've noticed that there are some remarkable people who can put others at their ease. My guess is that they do this by infecting others with calm. Calmness is a kind of virus. You can catch it, and you can pass it on. I think the calmness virus is transmitted on our breath.

People who can put others at their ease somehow get them to breathe more slowly, and more deeply. It may be that their stillness, their gentleness, or something that they do with their speech, communicates their own untroubled breathing. When we're with these people, we unconsciously pick up these rhythms and start to imitate them ourselves.

Shyness is a form of low-level panic. We feel panic as an intensely physical sensation. Our breathing becomes rapid and shallow, our pulses race, we begin to sweat. Our bodies are kick-starting the well-known "fight or flight" mechanism, a bundle of responses that's very handy if you're being threatened by a woolly mammoth, but a form of internal overkill in the modern business world.

Panic can be switched off with a number of tricks, the most important of which is slow steady breathing. Tension can be released by contracting, say, your leg muscles and then letting go. These panic removers can be used in diluted form to tackle shyness.

If you feel shyness creeping up on you, concentrate on slowing your breathing. You'll find that your thoughts also stop racing, and that you seem to have more time and space to experience the situation you're in. You'll become more aware of the room, and its sounds, without feeling any sense of threat.

With your breathing slowed down, you can now challenge your shyness with one simple question: What's the worst that could happen?

Imagine that I decide I'm going to march up to a stranger and ask him a question. What's the worst that could happen? Is he going to whip out a gun and shoot me through the head? I don't think so. Perhaps he might start yelling at me, and everyone will look at us. Okay, so what's the worst thing about that? People might think I'd said something rude to the man. And what's the worst thing about that? That I might be labelled as "a rude person" by a random bunch of strangers. So: can I live with that?

Yes, I can. If the very *worst* that can happen in a situation is that someone might shout at me, or some other people might mistakenly think ill of me, then I'll give it a shot. And, obviously, the very worst thing doesn't happen very often anyway.

I'm encouraging you to have many, many encounters. The arithmetic suggests that if you have a huge number of interactions, you will, now and then, experience the worst-case scenario. In my long career of meeting people, I've had a handful of such experiences. And here's the strange part: each one has strengthened me. I now *seek out these experiences*. I'm keen to be surprised by new "worst cases" – because I can't believe that this is the worst life can throw at me.

Someone doesn't feel like talking right now? That's okay: we all feel like that sometimes. It doesn't mean you should never again reach out.

Someone puts you down? That's okay: that's about *them*, not you. If the only way they can get their kicks is at the expense of warm people who reach out to them, then they're best left with their own little drama. You won't be able to help them out of it anyway.

Someone leads you on? That happens. People play games, but don't always tell the other players that they are in the game too. Your anger won't last for ever, you'll learn something along the way, and your antennae will be better tuned next time.

You'll get better at being shy by continuing to act shy. You'll get better at networking, and get more out of it, by continuing to network.

Reach out to people. Don't bother to pretend, or to present. People want to meet you, not some kind of act. If they wanted to watch an act, they'd go to a theatre. Nor do they want you to lay out your stall to them.

They don't want to be sold anything, converted to any point of view, or educated to degree level in some subject they've never thought about. They want to converse, which means they want to exchange ideas with you. They are looking for to-and-fro, not confrontation. They want to share themselves, not inspect you.

Some of the best networkers I know describe themselves as shy. I think what they mean is that they're self-conscious, and that they have a tendency to worry about what people will think of them. These are excellent indicators of a good networker. These feelings are symptoms that someone cares about other people, and that they want to communicate with others. And the fact that these people can express their belief that they are shy does, in a perverse way, neutralise their shyness. If you can say it, then it's not a problem.

I make myself available to everybody, including the supposedly shy. I encourage other networking leaders, such as club organisers and city Ecademy founders, to perform the same role.

That way, no matter what the make-up of the network at any time, there will be at least one person who's publicly committed to meeting with anyone who has a need. Life's a lot easier if everyone in the network takes on this role, and of course they do. But I think it's important that the leaders act as "the contact of last resort" for those who are finding their networking feet.

Your Face is Your Brand

The BBC once made a glossy TV series about the human face. John Cleese presented, and Liz Hurley lent her own features to some of the sections. The show proved one thing above all others: that despite its rather simple, standard geometric pattern, the human face is infinite in its variety, and its expressibility.

Just as nature never repeats a snowflake, it never replicates a face. And yet all faces are instantly recognisable to us as faces; and we are incredibly adept at reading them.

All faces are interesting, because all people are interesting. Your face is what people will remember of you. It is how they will index the mental information they store about you.

Your face isn't quite the same thing as your photograph. We experience faces as a rich collection of impressions, rather than a static image. My memories of well-loved faces include the way someone's eyes crinkle when he smiles, or the way someone's brow furrows when she is thinking. These are dynamic, impressionistic memories.

You burn these memories into the minds of the people you meet. They retain a visual memory of the way you make them feel.

Now, I'd be the last person to tell you that you can train your face to create the impression you want to leave. It's not possible unless you're a really fine actor – and if you're an actor, you should be on the stage. Networkers only need to be themselves. I don't want you to wear a mask, or try to cultivate some kind of "networking" expression that you can turn on and off at will.

But I do want you to bear in mind that when you network, you exist for others as more than pieces of lifeless information stored in a system, or the collection of words on your business card. You become an intimate part of their mental furniture. You have a role in their world.

For this reason, I discourage people from trying to develop complex brands around themselves. There was a fashion for this a few years back, though the many column inches written on the subject added up to little more than a general warning that people should expect to make their own way in the world, and therefore market themselves better to potential employers. I'm all for people taking responsibility for their lives, but you'll notice that I strongly believe we are on this journey together, and that we can therefore support each other's goals through networking.

If my view is correct, then trying to add a veneer of branding on to your own personality is not only unnecessary, it also lessens your value as networker by erecting a false barrier between yourself and other people. God has given you a brand already.

I can't leave the subject of personal branding without touching on my name – everybody else does. Power is the name of the family I was born into, and I'm proud of it. People often assume that I relish my name's association with, well, *power*. But, surprisingly enough, the surname "Power" means "poor" – or, just possibly, through a roundabout Norman reference to the town of Pois, "fish". Not so glamorous after all, then.

You don't need a smart, sophisticated brand to get yourself noticed in the networked world. You're known by your actions, and remembered by your face. Stay true to yourself, and be alive to the moment, and you'll be a valued member of the networked community, and a star to the people whose lives you touch.

Chapter 9
Networked Individualism

The more you give, the more you get back

I want to introduce you to yourself.

As a Power Networker, I make introductions all the time. I hope this is one of the most powerful introductions I ever have the pleasure to make.

Do I need to connect you with yourself? It's not as crazy as it sounds. The world has been changing so much over the last few years that it's become unrecognisable. And you've changed too. The person you need to be in the connected world has new habits of thought, new goals – and a renewed sense of individuality.

But I don't want you to just take my word for it. The new you I'm going to describe has emerged from the words of some deep and original thinkers. Before I introduce you to yourself, let me introduce you to them.

Digesting the Network Thinkers

I read as much as I can. I read a book every week. I read all types of books, but I take particular care to read the books that are influencing the way people think, act and communicate in the networked world.

The leading authors in these fields span disciplines as far-flung as history, economics, philosophy, psychology, biology, physics, mathematics and sociology, as well as the more obvious fields of business management and information technology.

I'm struck by the number of influential books streaming into the market around the concept of networking, and what networking means for our future lives. I take particular note of those thinkers who see the networked world as a political force that is changing the very fundamentals of our society.

Let's take a whistle-stop tour of these authors, and see how their ideas mesh with our mission to network. I hope this quick summary will be an appetiser for the books themselves, each of which is worthy of your best attention.

I'll start with *The Support Economy: Why Corporations Are Failing Individuals and The Next Episode of Capitalism* by Shoshana Zuboff and James Maxmin (Viking, 2002). Zuboff and Maxmin believe that the mass consumerism of the past is giving way to more personalised forms of service as suppliers move from transaction-based to relationship-based business models.

Their vision of a "distributed capitalism" humanises the economic machine, and – importantly – sees relationships as important in themselves rather than just as means to an end.

I am particularly impressed with the authors' phrase "psychological sovereignty", which they use to mean our rights to own our own minds. In the new economy, we are ourselves, not consumers or employees. It's also worth noting the sense of the authors' use of "support".

They mean that organisations need to *support* the lives that individuals choose to lead, rather than forcing them or enticing them down paths designed by the corporations.

I borrow the term "networked individualism" from Canadian academic Barry Wellman. Take a look at his paper *Little Boxes, Glocalization and Networked Individualism* (http://www.chass.utoronto.ca/~wellman/publications/littleboxes/littlebox.PDF). In Wellman's model, networked individualism is the third in a series of states, whereby people are connected in sparsely-knit networks with little regard to physical space. This is truly a new kind of social construct, where the people we know and trust best may be at the greatest distance. Psychological proximity has become more important than physical nearness. Our technologies enable this situation, and rather than enslaving us (as the standard nightmare of technologies suggests) they liberate us.

They enable us to be individuals again. It's nothing less than the smashing of dumb, mass markets. In the networked world, we each have a voice.

Robert D. Putnam's *Bowling Alone* (Touchstone, 2001) focuses on American society, but it makes fascinating reading for people from every country. Putnam starts with the thesis that American society is breaking down as fewer and fewer people participate in the family, the local community or even in the life of the nation. He adds a mass of research to detail the decline in participation, from parents' involvement with their children's schools, to – yes – trends in bowling.

Putnam charts how social capital can wither, showing over and over again how Americans have given up being "joiners" and so aided the diminishment of their civil society. The book contains a warning for us all.

David Weinberger's *Small Pieces Loosely Joined* (Perseus, 2002) is another book that has influenced my thinking. Weinberger – one of the authors of *The Cluetrain Manifesto* – studies how we use the net and how it has changed our world. In fact, Weinberger asserts that the world really has become the web. He describes we people as the "small pieces" connected in a series of "conversations" that are creating new markets and new opportunities. He also says the web is an "unnatural world" that we have created ourselves:

Suppose – just suppose – that the Web is a new world that we're just beginning to inhabit.

We don't know what's there and we don't know exactly what we need to find out. [...] The Web has no geography, no landscape. It has no distance. It has nothing natural in it. Common sense doesn't hold there, and uncommon sense hasn't yet emerged.

This chimes very closely with my experiences in Ecademy. The old common sense doesn't work, and we haven't yet agreed on any new common sense. This makes our newly connected world a very liberated place. As Weinberger says: "New worlds create new people."

Relationships, space, the web... This all sounds very human and political. But as we have seen, the new maths of networks is a neutral phenomenon that appears abundantly in nature. *Emergence: The Connected Lives of Ants, Brains, Cities, and Software* (Scribner, 2001) by Steven Johnson is a highly readable account of how order of stunning complexity and beauty emerges from simple actions. Ants, brains cities and software all emerge through individual actions that follow very simple rules.

Johnson's theme is the spontaneous appearance of intelligence within networks, a topic which has much to tell us about how human networks generate value.

There's a very approachable exploration of the incremental effects of networks in Malcolm Gladwell's *The Tipping Point: How Little Things Can Make a Big Difference* (Little, Brown, 2000). Gladwell looks at how ideas spread via "connectors" and "mavens" – people who like to network, and people who like to find and store information.

He uses real-life examples such as the "zero tolerance" policing policy pioneered in New York City, where concerted efforts to tackle minor crimes such as graffiti tagging led to reductions in major crimes like subway muggings.

For an alternative take on the "laws" of networking, read *Linked: The New Science of Networks* (Perseus, 2002) by Albert-László Barabási. Barabási has as many detractors as he has fans, but he's reporting as a researcher from the field and the connections he makes across a wide variety of different types of network are valuable in themselves.

The phenomenon that is often labelled "six degrees of separation" is explored in Duncan J. Watts's *Small Worlds* (Princeton University Press, 1999). As well as being a sociology professor at Columbia University, Watts is a Fellow at the Sante Fe Institute, the acknowledged world centre of research into complexity theory. In the book he examines the relationships between local and global effects in networks, covering economic and social networks as well as biological ones, physical ones and purely mathematical ones.

The short chains of associations that seem to occur spontaneously in networks create "small worlds" – as we say when we bump into close neighbours when we're on holiday on the other side of the world, or when we discover that we have a friend in common with a new, random acquaintance. Ecademy generates "small worlds" every day.

Watts's more recent book *Six Degrees: The Science of a Connected Age* (Norton, 2003) is also worth reading, not least for the excitement it communicates about the new maths of networking. You may also enjoy *Nexus: Small Worlds and the Groundbreaking Science of Networks* (Norton, 2002) by Mark Buchanan, an account of the emergence of "network science" as a field of study, beginning with a paper about coincidences published in *Nature* in 1998. (Here's a coincidence: we founded Ecademy in 1998.)

Howard Rheingold's *Smart Mobs: The Next Social Revolution* (Perseus, 2002) is the first book to take the new maths of networks and apply it to technologies beyond the desktop. Rheingold shows how connected, mobile devices allow people to find each other and organise into groups on the fly. The book has a lot to tell us about how consumer markets will develop, and also how networks like Ecademy will spread further into the communications fabric of everyday life as networking tools are used by more and more people.

Meet You

The books I've discussed in this chapter are the tip of a publishing iceberg. More books are being produced about network maths, network science, and network phenomena every day. The sheer weight of scholarship and commentary suggest that something significant is underway in the academic community.

But as networkers, we live and breathe this stuff every day. I am the maths: and so are you. The books give us light, but it's we networkers who make the heat.

Here's what you look like, in the illumination of these new discoveries.

You're an expert in at least one field, probably several. These fields sometimes feel like prisons, or end-points. But they're actually parts of your network, and they extend out along many paths.

Coincidences and connections spark around you. You constantly find yourself marvelling at the smallness of a world that seems to deliver so many spontaneous opportunities. The more you notice the coincidences, the more they seem to occur.

You're a novice in many more areas than you are an expert. The overwhelming extent of what you *don't* know excites you. You are always learning, always discovering.

You have an appetite for people. You love the surprises that people bring you. You love people's ability to understand you. You have a restless curiosity in what makes us all happy, what makes us tick.

You court randomness. You're not going to take the same train to the same job your whole life. You're going to explore everything that life has to offer you. You welcome the people and ideas that life strews in your path with such abandon. Because you are constantly open to random connections, you are never bored. Your world is never stale, but is constantly refreshed.

You let network maths work for you. That's why you aim for volume in your encounters. You cultivate your network, and your network sustains you.

You're a habitually good network citizen. You put people together. You reach out to people. You demonstrate, through your actions, how networkers live – in relaxed co-operation with each other.

You organise your networking activity using simple, but powerful tools. You exploit the Ecademy platform to enhance your network, and to make the most efficient use of it.

You are yourself. Others are themselves when they are around you.

You are an individual, *and* a part of a network. You feel no contradiction in these two states. You sense the connectedness of all people with each other, as well as their uniqueness. Your life and work are a celebration of our individuality, and our commonality.

You are the centre of a billion communities. You are the edge of a billion communities. You are the still point of a turning world, and you are a speck on its spinning rim.

You are more than the sum of your talents, more than the sum of your achievements, more than your inheritance, your education, or your luck. You are the product of the networked world you help to sustain. All its power is yours to command. Its power flows through, and to, you. The power exists through, and for, you.

Chapter 10
The Ten Steps of Networking

Many people have asked me to encapsulate my approach to power networking, and this set of ten steps is the result. These aren't commandments, nor are they laws. They are simply the ten sorts of things you need to do to become a successful networker, based on my personal experience, my observations of the growth of Ecademy, and the lessons I have learned from my contacts.

Put these ten steps to work for yourself, and networking will rapidly become second nature to you. These steps are simply habits of awareness. See yourself as someone who networks, and that's who you'll be.

Step One: Collect People

Be obsessed with collecting email addresses. In January 1999 I had 300 people in my Outlook contacts file. By January 2003 I had exactly 11,980.

This means I had been collecting people at the rate of 250 per month for 49 months. Believe me, this is seriously hard work. It takes around eighty to one hundred hours of personal networking online and offline each week.

I am not talking about buying a spam list for $199.00. I'm talking about real graft walking the world's pavements. In this time I have spoken in thirty countries, written four books and had 4,000 face-to-face meetings.

There's no escape from the arithmetic of networking. Put the time in, and build your networked world, person by person.

Step Two: Respect Geography

I spent four years working for Urban Science in Detroit where I learned to appreciate that most people spend 80% of their income within two miles of their front door.

This means that you should focus on your local network before your international network. It's easy to use email contacts to spread yourself widely, but true networking is about face-to-face meetings. Get a handle on networking in your neighbourhood, and you'll learn the skills and habits for networking on a wider scale. You'll also meet more potential value more quickly.

Five thousand of my personal contacts are in London. My partner Penny knows more than three hundred families in Farnham, our home town. My brother-in-law knows 5,000 people in the French city of Toulon, where he owns a hotel.

You can also use geography to deepen your network in pockets as you travel. If you travel as part of your job, research the area you're visiting before you go. Find out where people meet.

Look through Ecademists who live or work in the same area, and see if you can offer them anything while you're in their neighbourhood.

Eat with them, and get the sense of the places they live in. Your travels will become much more exciting as you see and learn much more than the isolated traveller sees.

Step Three: Start a Club

Think carefully about your topic, and then create a club for interested people. Your topic need not be business. We chose ebusiness at Ecademy, but it could have easily been Marketing, or Football, or Gliding, or Embroidery.

If you need help to decide on what club you should form, try using Marcus Buckingham and Donald O. Clifton's book *Now, Discover Your Strengths* (Free Press, 2002). This book concentrates on finding your strengths and playing to them. This can be a good way of finding out where your real passions lie, and also point you in the right direction for leading your club.

But you need to be first in the field. You also need to invest time in your club, recruiting members, creating interesting material, and organising events. Be first and go fast. Remember: *The winner of the game is the one with all the names.*

Step Four: Relax

Networking is a uniquely human activity. We're programmed to get along with each other, as well as to compete.

But we hear more about competition than co-operation. Our informal education in business, and the messages we absorb from the entertainment media, focus on conflict, and strategy, and quick-wittedness. Competing is all about adrenalin.

Networking isn't about sudden wins, but protracted relationships. We look for the strengths in our contacts, rather than looking for weaknesses in "opponents". Networking is a social activity, so successful networkers make sure that their encounters are comfortable, non-threatening, and conducive to sharing.

In many societies, alcohol is a social lubricant. It relaxes the natural inhibition, fear and apprehension that go along with meeting new people. I'm not promoting alcoholism, nor am I against those who don't drink. Alcohol is a depressant, and we have to use it wisely. But alcohol is one reason why effective networking often takes place in bars, over lunch or at parties.

Don't be afraid to use any technique for putting yourself and other people at ease. Your choice of venue can have a huge influence on an encounter, as can your dress code. Ecademists can be found networking in coffee shops, country pubs, motorway service stations and back gardens, as well as the more traditional venues in offices, hotels and clubs such as the Institute of Directors in London. Pick the level of formality that suits you, and you'll remove many of the unconscious barriers to successful networking.

Step Five: Go for Volume

You cannot build a "quality network". There is no such thing.

Think about it. If you could have a "quality network", then you'd be saying that some people are "quality", and others aren't. But that's not the way it works.

Pierre Danon is the CEO of BT's retail division. He is in a position of considerable power. And he is a great networker.

Ed Daniel is not the CEO of a large corporation. He is not in the same kind of position of power. But he is as great a networker as Pierre.

Do I shun Ed in favour of Pierre? Of course not. I'm not rating people on any kind of scale. And you would be foolish to do so.

Welcome everyone into your network: big or small, rich or poor, gay or straight, white or black. These things do not matter. These things are called prejudice. Prejudice stops you thinking, stops you listening, and ultimately stops you succeeding.

The only thing that matters in your network is volume. Make sure you meet twenty people per week, eighty people per month and 1,000 people per year. Commit these targets to memory.

You need volume in your network because *the money's in the links not the nodes*. Pierre and Ed have equal value in my network.

Either one can lead me to something I seek. None of us can tell what that something is, or when it will arise, or which path it will travel upon. In the world of networking, you do not know what you are seeking until you find it. You may be seeking a job, or knowledge, or some kind of transaction. Chances are, you will think you're seeking one goal but your network will produce other goals that are actually closer to your needs. But without volume in your network, there won't be enough links to produce the outcome you need.

Step Six: Listen for Link Words

When I am in meeting with someone, I ask "open questions". Open questions often start with one of the six great "w" questions: who, what, why, when, where and how. ("How" is an honorary "w" question, by long-standing tradition!) An open question doesn't contain any prompting for a particular answer.

Then I shut up, and listen, and make copious notes.

My notes are so copious that I consume a Moleskine notebook each and every month (see www.moleskine.com). Moleskine notebooks were used by the likes of Van Gogh and Hemingway – so they'll do for me. Try one for a month.

Notebooks also make great journals, providing sanctuary from the stresses of daily life. You might be using a PDA (Personal Digital Assistant) to organise your life, but that's unlikely to be the right tool for capturing your most personal thoughts. Use old-technology notebooks to write down your worries, your goals and your dreams.

Tell your notebook about your loneliness and your concerns. Challenge your negative thoughts as they occur. I'm an advocate of online tools: but there's something about the process of writing with a pen on paper, in your own private notebook, which connects directly with the head and heart.

It's vital that you listen for link words and write them down. You should collect fifty link words at each meeting. Do not leave the meeting until you have gathered those fifty link words. The meeting's not over until you have your fifty.

You must also review your notebooks at the end of each day so that your mind can ponder link words overnight. Great links will emerge in your mind. Never forget: *the money's in the links not the nodes.* So you must collect people, go for volume, and gather link words. This is the science of networks.

Be sure to re-read your notebooks at the end of every month, and at times when you're looking for a fresh thought or angle. Never throw your books away. They'll be useful when you write your memoirs. That's right: memoirs are for everybody. My mum's memoirs are fascinating, and I always wish my father had written his before he died in 1989. As you travel through the world, meeting people and listening hard to what they have to say, and helping to connect them with each other, you are weaving a fascinating story of life in our massively connected world. Those notes are to be treasured. They are as valuable as your family photographs.

They are recording your life, your growth, your development and your richness. They become a testament to the good you have done in the world.

Step Seven: Create Matches

Once you have had time to ponder the links words you have collected, you must make connections. Be a matchmaker. Use the Ecademy member directory to put people together.

Don't think about "what's in it for me". Think about what might be in it for them. Then simply make the connection and move on. The more connections you make, the larger your network becomes. Not every connection generates financial wealth for you. In fact, only some one in fifty connections generates direct wealth for you.

But the remaining forty-nine connections generate reputation, knowledge, kindness, politeness, peace of mind and many free lunches.

This is wealth also. Happiness is wealth. Friends are wealth. Networks are wealth.

Do not be blinded by your need for financial transactions. They're a small part of the picture. The billionaire oil magnate and philanthropist John D. Rockefeller, Jr. said: "The poorest man I know is the man who has nothing but money."

Step Eight: Disturb Your Comfort Zone

That's right: do something that disrupts your normal, comfortable pattern.

None of us likes doing this. But we're all better off for doing it. It means reading books you don't like, as well as the ones you do. It means reading magazines designed for a different target group. It means going to events and networking sessions you consider irrelevant. It means putting yourself in the wrong places, at the wrong times, with the wrong people.

What is the value of Step Eight? The point is to release your subconscious mind, to open it to novel materials that may reveal new links. You are already creating volume, listening for link words and letting your conscious and unconscious mind process those links. By disturbing your comfort zone, you enlarge your mind's processing capacity. It's like magnifying the volume of your network, or – more closely – having more than one brain on the job.

And sometimes you will discover that the tastes you thought you always had weren't quite right. Or that some group you dismissed as irrelevant has something sensible to say after all.

Many people ignore Step Eight. But it is a powerful way of accelerating and deepening your networking activity. Disturbing your comfort zone on a regular basis is a sure-fire way to keep learning and growing. Surprise yourself!

Step Nine: Read

Yes, not only am I an evangelist of the online economy who writes with a pen in notebooks, I'm also a modern communicator who believes in the ancient technology of reading.

Reading is the key skill of the new economy. It's not "computer literacy", which just means the ability to use an interface. Being able to use technology will help you find the information you need, but you need to apply your brain before that information is any use in the real world.

No time to read? Groucho Marx said: "I find television very educational. Every time someone switches it on, I go into another room and read a good book."

I read a book each and every week. Make sure you read regularly, even if you simply re-read your notebooks (see Step Six). Read offline, read online, read on the loo, read on the train, read on the plane, read in bed. Read, read, and read.

Did I mention that you should read?

Step Ten: Manage your Reputation

Take care of your reputation. Guard it both online and off. Your reputation isn't the same as your character, but it is your character's proxy. In other words, in the social world, your reputation *is* you. And your reputation will outlive you.

If you make an error that affects your reputation online or off, apologise and make amends immediately. Keep your reputation in good repair. Think of it as a dimension of your health. Think of it as your place in history.

A simple and direct way of building your reputation is to gather written testimonials. It surprises me how few people ask for positive feedback in this way. Yet we are all interested in objective feedback from people on how someone has performed, or how she has added value. When something goes right, ask the people involved if they'll write a few words saying so. More often than not, they'll be happy to oblige. Putting their feedback in writing is an excellent means of sealing a transaction or a relationship, and costs nothing. People like to have their opinions known.

Never forget that *your face is your brand*. Spread that face around the place and keep it looking good. Exercise, eat and sleep well. You are your most valuable business tool, so invest in your upkeep and development.

Chapter 11

Networking For Life

Live The Life

In this final chapter I look at two very practical and personal networking issues.

The first of these issues is how value is shared by networkers in real, hard-cash terms through Ecademy's referrals programme. The programme is one pointer towards a near future in which networking underpins our economy. And that's the essence of this chapter's second issue: the removal of our traditional economic foundations.

Incomes in the western world are threatened by 50% deflation due to competition from lower-cost regions. The average westerner is ill prepared for the rapid decline in income that will hit us all during the next decades. As skilled labour continues to move to India, China, South Africa, Malaysia and Eastern Europe, people in the "old world" are finding their own market value plummeting.

Networking can save us from this fate, creating an alternative economic engine that will outstrip the traditional alternative.

I believe Ecademy is the harbinger of the new networked economy – its first living, breathing organism.

I believe you'll want to take advantage of everything Ecademy has to offer, integrating your membership within a rich and satisfying life dedicated to – and made possible by – networking.

I know you're already part of the great network: the fact that you hold this book in your hands tells me that. Now you're ready to make networking the central activity in your life.

Value in Flow

Networks generate value in unexpected ways. That's their beauty. However, there are also ways in which networks can express and direct value in more explicit ways. Ecademy's referrals programme is a great example of an explicit networking value flow.

Ecademy's referrals programme was launched in May 2003. It's designed to reward people who help the membership to grow, and in particular the number of Power Networkers. The programme's rewards come in the form of real money.

When a Power Networker brings a new Power Networker into Ecademy, either by invitation or via a club or SIG that he runs, part of the new member's subscription is returned to the introducer.

It's a simple commission scheme that ensures our members share in the growth they help to generate.

The programme is administered through the Ecademy platform, so there's no painful form-filling or claims process.

But it goes beyond that. Unlike most commission schemes, Ecademy continues to pay referral fees for the membership lifetime of both parties.

This gives a continuous income stream for introducers, and creates an added incentive for Power Networkers to nurture their clubs and contribute content to the site.

The referrals programme uses network maths to set up a virtuous cycle. It makes growing your network more fun, while using the notion that there's more to share when the cake keeps growing. The full details of the scheme, and how you can get on board today, are on the Ecademy site at www.ecademy.com.

I'm reminded of a phrase that's familiar to entrepreneurs: "shared risk, shared reward". This is an approach to shared projects where all the parties recognise that they are exposed to risks during the development of the business, but that they are equally entitled to the rewards they are working for. In practical terms, it might mean that a supplier foregoes some or all of his payment in return for shares in the new enterprise.

Our referrals programme has the same quality of shared endeavour. But the similarity ends there. Ours is a "shared reward, shared reward" scheme. We've designed it so that everyone wins.

Let me make one thing crystal clear. This is *not* a network marketing scheme. Members of the programme do *not* sell anything to anyone. We don't give you a box of brushes or a case of shampoo and a rousing song to sing.

The programme is a logical evolutionary step for Ecademy. We already had the functionality to enable members to invite people to join, and we publish statistics on the numbers of new members who join through this route. We built the functionality to enable clubs and SIGs.

What the referrals programme does is to add some economic spice to these functions. The programme directs some of the network's value back to those who initiated it.

More significantly, the programme lets us do something truly amazing for our members. It lets them start earning a living from networking right here, right now. That's something we've all got to do. And *right now* is the latest any of us can leave it.

Replacing Lost Jobs

Jobs are being drained from our economy. The western world's traditional jobs are all being relocated to lower-cost economies. We're now used to this idea in the heavy industries like steel or shipbuilding. We've even got used to the idea that advanced electronic products come from the east rather than the west. But we're still attached to the idea that "knowledge work" belongs in Europe or America. Now even that idea is under attack.

Jobs in information technology and associated clerical and administrative areas are steadily moving abroad. Call centres, which have been the only white-collar growth area in the UK for more than a decade, are being closed as staff in India take over the headsets. Large-scale data entry jobs are subcontracted to the Far East. Programmers in India and China develop complex business systems for European and American clients at a fraction of the prices charged by home-grown talent. The new communications channels that have shrunk our world and enlarged our market opportunities have also massively increased competition. Being talented and local is no longer enough. The knowledge worker of today has to offer a lot more.

The immediate threat is a 50% cut in average income as skilled labour continues to move to India, China, South Africa, Malaysia and Eastern Europe. And that's a prediction about *average* incomes. For millions of individuals, the true effect will be more brutal. All kinds of people in the "old world" will find their own market value plummeting.

What will our displaced knowledge workers do? Futurologists once prophesied an era of "leisure" for those skilled and unskilled workers who would be replaced by automated processes. That future came about, although "leisure" wasn't an appropriate word for the widespread unemployment that tore apart communities and took away individuals' self-esteem.

One answer may be to concentrate on the highest value knowledge industries. Commentators point to British successes in design, fashion and music and our lucky inheritance of the world's common language, English. And maybe this is a route to wealth for some people. If we can't all be systems analysts, perhaps a few of us can make it as screenwriters.

The flaw in this thinking is that it's... *top*-ist. Not everyone can make a hit record, or direct a blockbuster movie. And even if we *can* all be famous for fifteen minutes, we need to be earning a living for our entire lives, not one brief flash.

You can no longer compete on skill. What you know is no longer a precious commodity. In fact, your knowledge has become a kind of currency that you need to keep acquiring and spending, rather than hoarding.

But there *is* something that we can all do – something that will drive the economy, creating new industries and new value streams. That something is networking.

The only advantage we in the west have is our ability to connect with each other. We are blessed with mature infrastructure, healthcare, education and with stable political and legal institutions. We are privileged to be able to agonise over the shape of mineral water bottles, rather than worry about the purity of the water from our town's only standpipe. But our competitors will acquire all these benefits in time.

They, like us, will take the rewards of industrialisation for granted. And they will continue to unleash their own knowledge power on our markets.

However, networkers do more than turn ideas into products or services. They actually *form markets*. New markets emerge from the activity of networking. These new markets may in turn become the focus of external competition. But their formation and control remain with their members.

Let's take a striking example. The American Society of Association Executives (ASAE; www.asaenet.org) is known as "the association of associations". The society exists to promote the value of voluntary organisations and support the individuals who lead them. ASAE has been operating since 1920 and has 25,000 members who in turn manage leading trade, professional, and philanthropic associations. Through those associations, ASAE represents a community of more than 287 million people worldwide. Crucially, vendors make up a vital part of this enormous community. These vendors offer products and services to the community.

Associations in the United States are, when aggregated, the largest market for many high-value products and services. They are the biggest buyers of car rentals, flights and hotel reservations. This is because associations run regular conventions – networking events. Many Americans combine their attendance at conventions with family holidays, showing once more how networking blurs the line between work and life.

Another example of the incredible economic power of networks is the AARP. The AARP (formerly known as the American Association of Retired Persons; www.aarp.org) was founded in 1958 and now has more than 35 million members. The organisation was founded to represent the interests of older people, but stresses that "healthy aging requires an early start". About half of AARP's members are working full- or part-time. Nearly a third of the members are under the age of 60; 46% are aged between 60 and 74, and 21% are 75 or older. The organisation says: "The collective strength of our membership enables us to serve the broader community, improving the quality of life for people as they get older."

One of AARP's roles, alongside education, community involvement and advocacy, is the provision of products and services to the membership. It is the US's largest pension provider. It provides a wide range of services including healthcare and insurance, as well as discounts on hotels, car rentals, holidays and even consumer products.

The AARP is a fine example of the economic potential of networks. The organisation has developed a layer of economic benefits that go *alongside* its core functions of bringing people together and supporting their interests.

The members' benefits have grown organically with the growth of the network. The network has formed itself into a market.

American associations grew in a way that should be familiar to us by now. They were built around publishing, events and local chapters. The publications focused on relevant advice and entertaining content, just as Ecademy's website and publications continue to do. The local chapters became the engine of growth, just like Ecademy's local cells. And the growth curves for organisations like ASAE and AARP are similar to those I project for Ecademy.

I'm indebted to Ecademist Freddie McMahon who showed me these parallels, and who has called Ecademy "the world's first 21st century association". We're proving the association model, but combining it with the powerful communications and computing technology we now have at our disposal. We're following the logic of shared interests, but adding the new insights of network science to encourage the emergence of new centres of interest.

We all have one job in common: to create the new jobs that will replace the old jobs. This means that we must come together to generate and supply new markets. Networking is the answer to the problems of skills-based economics, and knowledge-based economics. It is the medium through which our future prosperity will be born.

The Calling

This book has been about exposing my life. I've tried to communicate what it's like to be a networker, and how networkers see the world. I hope I've managed to dispel a few myths about networking and to show that it's not just for the few.

In fact, I hope I've made you see that networking had better be for everybody. Networking is what will carry each and every one of us forward. It will generate our incomes, and provide our pensions. It already provides us with more enhanced opportunities, greater involvement in our community, and more sheer delight in life than any other activity I know. What else combines good companionship, lifelong learning *and* an income? Networking is already giving us all these benefits, for minimum outlay and without any special training. And, as each day goes by, networking is becoming the supreme business and lifestyle activity. It's an activity that is subsuming everything else.

Take the business world. Take marketing. The best-value marketing approach today is viral marketing, where customers essentially inform each other of a product or service. That's networking.

Or look at the retail sector. Loyalty cards attract us to particular supermarkets or aggregations of retailers, and retain us as customers. These programmes recognise and reward our buying patterns. They get us to change our habits, making us use alternative fuel companies or pharmacies. That's networking.

Take a look on the streets and try to figure out who's in charge of an anti-globalisation rally, or an anti-war protest. There's no one in charge: there's no top. These movements emerge spontaneously from smaller groups, which themselves form around distinct issues. That's networking.

Wherever you look today, you can see the power of networking. And when you consider how it's the networkers who get things done, it starts to be obvious that we all ought to be doing it. In fact, we all *are* networking. Even those people who swear blind that they aren't.

Have you ever been confused or bored by the advertising for a type of product you're interested in buying? Perhaps you asked a trusted friend for her advice. That's networking. If you looked up *Which?* then you followed the advice of a supreme network, the Consumer's Association. That's networking too. You're a part of this thing already.

There are some conditions that I'll accept make a non-networker. If you can introduce me to someone who fulfils all these criteria, then I'll eat my hat, and everyone else's hat too. (But then, if you can introduce this person to me, then they must be networked!)

Here's what the earth's last remaining non-networker looks like. He has never asked someone else a question, and never will. He knows everything he will ever need to know, and was born with that knowledge. He has a document signed and sealed by every governmental and supra-governmental organisation in the world promising that the business environment will never change and entitling him to a lifetime, index-linked income. He is an island.

Networking is, above all, an expression of trust. It's the embodiment of our shared recognition of our common humanity. So long as people value each other, they will network.

Clearly, I want you to raise your networking activity to a higher plane. I know you already network, and that you enjoy it. But I want you to be a supreme networker. I want you to be a Power Networker. And I want you to be a better-than-Thomas-Power networker too. Surpass me. Leave me in the dust. Show me the way to a world of even greater volume and diversity. Multiply my links. *Expand my life*.

Do it for yourself, do it for me, do it for us. Do it for all of us.

It's never been clearer that we've reached a historic moment in the development of human kind. Join that moment. Live The Life.

Beyondword

We've all read books with forewords, and even some books with afterwords. This is a beyondword. It's a set of messages intended to carry you forward on your journey.

I want to leave you with some simple ideas that I hope will reverberate in your life long after you have put this book down. Then, when we meet – as we will surely do, somehow, someday – we'll both instantly know that we chose together a common way: the way of networking.

I'm hoping that these last words will help add a further dimension to the serendipity that we're all striving to accelerate. And that dimension is an element of spiritual recognition. As we all, dedicated and habitual networkers to the very last of us, strive to connect with each other, to *collect* each other, I hope we'll recognise through some of these final ideas an emotional closeness that we bring to each encounter. It'll be as if we already know each other.

That's the dream. Let's see if it works.

Affirmations

These are the statements I use to keep myself on-track as a networker. You might want to use them yourself, or adapt them.

They sum up my personal philosophy of networking, and networking's connection to my deepest beliefs. They also remind me how networking is not simply a collection of techniques but a habit of mind and aspect of living.

- I accept responsibility for all outcomes.

- I remain patient for the outcomes of my desires, trusting the universe to bring results.

- I am learning to let go as I set course for a higher plane.

- I have no trouble embracing uncertainty and ambiguity.

- I am open-minded and approachable on all subjects by all people.

- I am willing to be known and share my knowledge with others.

- I have good antennae and am alert to tiny signals.

- I recognise that all thoughts, even minor ones, have consequences.

- I am not attached to the past or how things should turn out.

- I adapt quickly to errors and mistakes.

- I forgive myself when selfishness or delusion creep back into my life.

- I fulfil myself through unlimited inspiration, creativity and discovery.

- I make connections.

- I can see the meaning in chance events.

- My greatest strength is imagination.

- My biggest hurdle is self-importance.

- I want to feel connected to the whole.

- I want my life to have meaning.

- I want to be free of restrictions.

- Everyday I reinforce my intentions.

Networking is...

a path

a making of paths

a behaviour

a guide for behaviour

a belief

a process of believing

Networking is...

community

family

individuality

interdependence

diversity

commonality

Networking is...

a way of looking at the world

a way of being in the world

a way of being of the world

Networking is...

for a rainy day

for a sunny day

for every day

for the driven

for everyone

for fun

for life

Thank You

Thank you for sharing this part of life's journey with me. I hope you have taken ideas from this book, and taken heart. I hope you're ready to embrace networking as a way of life, and to enjoy the many new connections you're about to start making. I hope, through these pages, we have connected.

I look forward to the conversations we will have, with each other and through each other, in the growing network that we share. And I wish you great luck and god speed as you forge your own networking adventure.

Required Reading

These are the books and articles that have influenced my thinking about networking over the last few years. I've mentioned many of them briefly in this book. Since I spend all my time doing networking, I get a lot of enjoyment from reading about networking, and discussing it. All of these sources will provide you with extra gristle to chew on, as well as adding different voices to the discussion.

Howard Baker, *One Minute Meeting* (Forum, 1994)
Wayne E. Baker, *Achieving Success Through Social Capital: Tapping Hidden Resources in Your Personal and Business Networks* (Jossey-Bass, 2000)
Wayne E. Baker, *Networking Smart: How to Build Relationships for Personal and Organizational Success* (McGraw-Hill, 1994)
Drew Banks and Kim Daus, *Customer.Community: Unleashing the Power of Your Customer Base* (Jossey Bass Wiley, 2002)
Albert-László Barabási, *Linked: The New Science of Networks* (Perseus, 2002)
Alexander Bard and Jan Soderqvist, *Netocracy: The New Power Elite and Life after Capitalism* (Reuters, 2002)
Brian Bates and John Cleese, *The Human Face* (BBC, 2001)

Peter J. Bentley, *Digital Biology* (Simon & Schuster, 2002)

Lillian D. Bjorseth, *Breakthrough Networking: Building Relationships That Last* (Duoforce, 2nd edition 2003)

Susan Blackmore and Richard Dawkins (Foreword), *The Meme Machine* (Oxford University Press, 1999)

Bela Bollobas, *Random Graphs* (Cambridge University Press, 2001)

Roger Bootle, *The Death of Inflation: Surviving and Thriving in the Zero Era* (Nicholas Brealey, 1996)

Mark Buchanan, *Nexus: Small Worlds and the Groundbreaking Science of Networks* (Norton, 2002)

Mark Buchanan, *Ubiquity: The Science of History... or Why the World Is Simpler Than We Think* (Crown, 2001)

Marcus Buckingham and Donald O. Clifton, *Now, Discover Your Strengths* (Free Press, 2002)

Roger Camrass and Martin Farncombe, *The Atomic Corporation: A Rational Proposal for Uncertain Times* (Capstone, 2001)

Manuel Castells, *The Internet Galaxy: Reflections on the Internet, Business and Society* (Oxford University Press, 2002)

Manuel Castells, *The Power of Identity* (Blackwell, 1997)

Hilton Catt and Patricia Scudamore, *30 Minutes to Improve Your Networking Skills* (Kogan Page, 2000)

Shelle Rose Charvet, *Words That Change Minds: Mastering the Language of Influence* (Kendall/Hunt, 1997)

Deepak Chopra, *The Seven Spiritual Laws of Success: A Practical Guide to the Fulfilment of Your Dreams* (Bantam, 1996)

Deepak Chopra, *Golf for Enlightenment: Seven Lessons for the Game of Life* (Random House, 2003)

Deepak Chopra, *How to Know God: The Soul's Journey into the Mystery of Mysteries* (Rider, 2001)

R. H. Coase, *The Firm, the Market, and the Law* (University of Chicago Press, 1988)

Mick Cope, *Personal Networking: How to Make Your Connections Count* (Financial Times Prentice Hall, 2002)

Stephen R. Covey, *7 Habits of Highly Effective People*, (Simon & Schuster, 1999)

Thomas H. Davenport and John C. Beck, *The Attention Economy: Understanding the New Currency of Business* (Harvard Business School Press, 2002)

Ross Dawson, *Living Networks: Leading Your Company, Customers, and Partners in the Hyper-Connected Economy* (Financial Times/Prentice Hall, 2002)

Cory Doctorow, *Down and Out in the Magic Kingdom* (Tor, 2003)

Donna Fisher, *Professional Networking for Dummies* (John Wiley, 2001)

Donna Fisher and Sandy Vilas, *Power Networking: 59 Secrets for Personal and Professional Success* (National Book Network, 2000)

Thomas L. Friedman, *The Lexus and the Olive Tree* (Anchor/Doubleday, 2000)

John Kenneth Galbraith, *A History Of Economics: The Past as the Present* (Penguin, 1988)

John Kenneth Galbraith, *The Affluent Society* (Penguin, 1999)

Michael E. Gerber, *The E Myth Revisited: Why Most Small Businesses Still Don't Work and What You Can Do About Yours* (HarperCollins, 1995)

Melissa Giovagnoli and Jocelyn Carter-Miller, *Networlding: Building Relationships and Opportunities for Success* (Jossey-Bass, 2000)

James H. Gilmore and B. Joseph Pine II, *The Experience Economy* (Harvard Business School Press, 1999)

Malcolm Gladwell, *The Tipping Point: How Little Things Can Make a Big Difference* (Little, Brown, 2000)

Marc Gobe, *Emotional Branding: The New Paradigm for Connecting Brands to People* (Allworth, 2001)

Seth Godin, *Unleashing the Ideavirus* (Hyperion, 2001)

Seth Godin, *Permission Marketing: Turning Strangers into Friends, and Friends into Customers* (Simon and Schuster, 1999)

Mark Granovetter and Richard Swedberg, *The Sociology of Economic Life* (Westview, 2001)

Mark S. Granovetter, "The Strength of Weak Ties", *American Journal of Sociology*, v78, n6, May 1973, 1360-1380;
http://web.media.mit.edu/~tanzeem/cohn/granovetter73.pdf

John Hagel III, *Out of the Box: Strategies for Achieving Profits Today and Growth Tomorrow Through Web Services* (Harvard Business School Press, 2002)

Peta Heskell, *Flirt Coach* (HarperCollins, 2001)

Napoleon Hill, *Think and Grow Rich* (Fawcett, 1990)

Dee Hock, *Birth of the Chaordic Age* (Berrett-Koehler, 1999)

John H. Holland, *Hidden Order: How Adaptation Builds Complexity* (Perseus, 1996)

Spencer Johnson, *Who Moved My Cheese?: An Amazing Way to Deal with Change in Your Work and in Your Life* (Vermillion, 1999)

Steven Johnson, *Emergence: The Connected Lives of Ants, Brains, Cities, and Software* (Scribner, 2001)

Leil Lowndes, *How to Make Anyone Fall in Love with You: 85 Proven Techniques for Success* (Harper Collins, 1997)

Ivan R. Misner and Don Morgan, *Masters of Networking: Building Relationships for Your Pocketbook and Soul* (National Book Network, 2000)

Geoffrey Moore, *Crossing the Chasm: Marketing and Selling Technology Products to Mainstream Customers* (HarperCollins, 1991)

Geoffrey Moore, *Living on the Fault Line: Managing for Shareholder Value in the Age of the Internet* (Capstone, 2000)

James Moore, *The Death of Competition: Leadership and Strategy in the Age of Business Ecosystems* (John Wiley, 1996)

John Milton Fogg, *Conversations with the Greatest Networker in the World* (Prima Lifestyles, 2000)

John Milton Fogg, *The Greatest Networker in the World* (Prima Lifestyles, 1997)

Harold J. Morowitz, *The Emergence of Everything: How the World Became Complex* (Oxford University Press, 2002)

Paul Ormerod, *Butterfly Economics: A New General Theory of Economic and Social Behaviour* (Faber and Faber, 1999)

Thomas Paine, *The Rights of Man* (Dover, 1999)

Norman Vincent Peale, *The Power of Positive Thinking* (Hutchinson, 1999)

Thomas Power and George Jerjian, *Ecosystem: Living the 12 Principles of Networked Business* (Financial Times Prentice Hall, 2001)

Robert D. Putnam, *Bowling Alone* (Touchstone, 2001)

Howard Rheingold, *Smart Mobs: The Next Social Revolution* (Perseus, 2002)

Susan RoAne, *How to Work a Room: The Ultimate Guide to Savvy Socializing in Person and Online* (HarperResource, 2000)

Emanuel Rosen, *The Anatomy of Buzz: How to Create Word-Of-Mouth Marketing* (Doubleday, 2002)

Michael Rothschild, *Bionomics: Economy as Ecosystem* (Henry Holt, 1995)

Tim Sanders, *Love is the Killer App: How to Win Business and Influence Friends* (Crown, 2002)

Doc Searls and David Weinberger, *World of Ends: What the Internet Is and How to Stop Mistaking It for Something Else*; http://worldofends.com/

John Seely Brown and Paul Duguid, *The Social Life of Information* (Harvard Business School Press, 2000)

Peter M. Senge, *The Fifth Discipline: The Art and Practice of the Learning Organization* (Random House, 1993)

Carl Shapiro and Hal Varian, *Information Rules: A Strategic Guide to the Network Economy* (Harvard Business School Press, 1998)

Oz Shy, *The Economics of Network Industries* (Cambridge University Press, 2001)

Joseph T. Sinclair, *EBay the Smart Way: Selling, Buying and Profiting on the Web's #1 Auction Site* (Amacom, 2001)

Adam Smith, *The Wealth of Nations* (Random House, 2000)

Mike Southon and Chris West, *The Beermat Entrepreneur: Turn Your Good Ideas into a Great Business* (Prentice Hall, 2002)

Carole Stone, *Networking: The Art of Making More Friends* (Vermillion, 2001)

Steven Strogtaz, *Sync: The Emerging Science of Spontaneous Order* (Hyperion, 2003)

Nassim Nicholas Taleb, *Fooled by Randomness: The Hidden Role of Chance in the Markets and in Life* (Texere Publishing, 2001)

Graham Tanaka, *Digital Deflation: Solving the Mystery of the New Economy* (McGraw-Hill, 2003)

David Taylor, *The Naked Leader* (Capstone, 2002)

Mark C. Taylor, *The Moment of Complexity: Emerging Network Culture* (University of Chicago Press, 2002)

Michael Treacy and Fred Wiersema, *The Discipline of Market Leaders: Choose Your Customers, Narrow Your Focus, Dominate Your Market* (Perseus, 1997)

M. Mitchell Waldrop, *Complexity: The Emerging Science at the Edge of Order and Chaos* (Touchstone, 1992)

Neale Donald Walsch, *Conversations with God: An Uncommon Dialogue* (Hodder Mobius, 1997)

Duncan J. Watts, *Small Worlds* (Princeton University Press, 1999)

Duncan J. Watts, *Six Degrees: The Science of a Connected Age* (Norton, 2003)

David Weinberger, *Small Pieces Loosely Joined* (Perseus, 2002)

Stephen Wolfram, *A New Kind of Science* (Wolfram Media, 2002)

Zig Ziglar, *Network Marketing for Dummies* (John Wiley, 2000)
Shoshana Zuboff and James Maxmin, *The Support Economy: Why Corporations Are Failing Individuals and The Next Episode of Capitalism* (Viking, 2002)